Web Design Index 8

Compiled & Edited by Günter Beer

The Pepin Press

AMSTERDAM & SINGAPORE

The **Web Design Index** has become the industry standard for tracking and cataloguing innovations in web design. The sites featured in this series are selected from those nominated on the webdesignindex.org website, from the portfolios of designers who have recently received web awards and from the work of new designers who have received recognition for innovative design. The selection process focuses not only on visual design but also on functionality and the innovative use of new technologies.

The URL is indicated for each website. The names of those involved in the design and programming of the sites are listed as follows:

design	D
coding	C
production	P
agency	A
designer's contact address	M

A CD-ROM containing all the pages featured in this book can be found inside the back cover. Movie previews are also included for all websites which contain animation or movies. The CD allows you to view the site design without accessing the internet and acts as an archive should the websites be taken offline. If you prefer seeing the entire website, hyperlinks on the CD will take you there directly.

Submissions & recommendations

Each year, The Pepin Press publishes new editions of two leading reference books in web design: **Web Design Index** and **Web Design Index by Content**. If you would like to submit or recommend designs for consideration, please complete the submissions form at www.webdesignindex.org.

The Pepin Press

For more information on The Pepin Press or to order from our selection of publications on design, fashion, popular culture, visual reference and ready-to-use images, please visit www.pepinpress.com

序文

Web Design Indexは、最先端のウェブ・デザインのトレンドを把握するための業界基準となりました。今回は、ウェブ関連の賞を受賞し「webdesignindex.org」のサイトでとりあげられたデザイナー、および斬新なデザインで注目されている新進気鋭のデザイナーによるサイトを紹介しています。視覚的なデザインだけでなく、機能性を重視したサイトや新しいテクノロジーを取り入れたサイトを厳選して紹介しています。

本書には、各サイトのURL、及びデザイナーとプログラマーの名前も載せています。表記方法は以下のとおりです。

D   デザイン
C   コーディング
P   プロダクション
A   エージェンシー
M   デザイナーの連絡先

附録のCD-ROMには、本書に紹介されているサイトがすべて収録されています。アニメーションやムービーを含むサイトも動画で見ることができます。CDに収録されたサイトは、インターネットに接続しなくても見ることができます。また、実際のサイトがインターネット上から削除されてもアーカイブとして利用し、いつでも希望するサイトを見ることができます。実際のサイトにもすぐにアクセスできるよう、CDにはハイパーリンクを設けました。

ウェブサイトの自薦・他薦

Pepin Pressは、ウェブデザイン業界の人気参考書、「Web Design Index」と「Web Design Index by Content」の改訂版を毎年出版しています。自分のウェブサイトを掲載ご希望の場合、また推薦なさりたいサイトがある場合には、www.webdesignindex.orgにアクセスしてお申し込みください。

The Pepin Press

Pepin Pressは、デザインやファッション、ポップ・カルチャーなどについて多様な出版物や、すぐにそのまま使えるイメージ素材などを出版しています。当社の出版物やイメージ素材について、詳しい情報をお知りになりたい方、あるいは当社の商品をご注文なさりたい方は、www.pepinpress.comにアクセスしてください。

【网页设计索引】已成为行内人士追踪及编录崭新网页设计潮流的标准。本系列提及的网页全部选自 webdesignindex.org ，展示最近获奖的网页设计师及其创意受到认同的新进设计师的作品。评选的准则不单集中在视觉设计上，亦在网页的功能性及新科技的创意运用上。

本书列出每个网页的统一资源定位符(URL)。网页的设计和编写程式的人员名单，分列如下：

设计	D
编码	C
制作	P
代理	A
设计人员的联系地址	M

本书的封底附上一只 CD-ROM 光碟，内里包含书中提及的所有网页，以及网页附有的动画或电影的预告片段。这只 CD-ROM 光碟能让您无须上网便能参阅精选的网页设计。就算网页一旦暂停服务，CD-ROM 光碟亦能充作资料库作存档之用。为了方便您浏览整个网站的内容，光碟亦提供了超链接。

投稿及推荐

Web Design Index(网页设计索引) 及 Web Design Index by Content (网页设计索引 – 主题篇) 这两部参考书籍，在网页设计业内带著领导的地位。The Pepin Press每年均会为这两部书推出新订版。若阁下有意把设计投稿或作推荐，请到www.webdesignindex.org填写投稿表格。

The Pepin Press

若阁下需要更多关于The Pepin Press的资料，或想订购本社有关设计、时装、流行文化、视觉参考及现成图像的刊物，请到www.pepinpress.com查阅本社的网页。

소개

웹 디자인 인덱스는 이미 최신 작품을 추적하고 알아보는 웹 디자인 업계의 표준 출판물이 됩니다. 이 시리즈에 선택하는 작품은 모두 **webdesignindex.org** 웹 사이트에서 추천한 것입니다. 이 것들은 모두 최근에 웹 디자인 상을 받은 디자이너와 디자인 혁신면에서 인정을 받은 새로운 디자이너의 작품들입니다. 작품 선택 과정에서 시각적인 디자인 뿐만 아니라 기능과 새로운 기술의 사용도 선택의 주안점이 됩니다.

책에는 각 사이트의 URL이 표시되어 있습니다. 사이트의 디자인 및 프로그래밍 관련 명칭은 다음과 같이 표기되어 있습니다.

D   디자인
C   코딩
P   제작
A   대행사
M   디자이너 연락처

CD 한장을 뒤 표지에 붙여서 이 책의 모든 내용을 포함합니다. 애니메이션이나 영화를 포함한 웹사이트의 영화 예고편도 포함합니다. 이 **CD**는 웹 사이트가 오프라인일 때 아카이브가 될 수 있어서 **CD**를 사용하면 인터넷을 접속하지 않아도 사이트 디자인을 볼 수 있습니다. 전체 웹사이트를 보려면 하이퍼 링크를 클릭하여 직접 방문할 수 있습니다.

제안 및 추천

해마다 Pepin Press는 웹 디자인의 두 가지 주요 참고 서적, Web Design Index (웹 디자인 인덱스) 및 Web Design Index by Content (내용별 웹 디자인)를 새로운 버전으로 출판합니다. 생각하고 있는 디자인을 제출하거나 추천하시려면 www.webdesignindex.org에서 제출 양식을 작성하시기 바랍니다.

The Pepin Press

디자인, 패션, 대중문화, 영상 자료 및 기성 이미지와 관련된 수많은 Pepin Press의 출판물 및 주문에 대한 자세한 내용은 www.pepinpress.com을 방문하시기 바랍니다.

Einleitung

Der **Web Design Index** hat sich zum Standardwerk für die Katalogisierung von innovativem Webdesign entwickelt. Die in diesem Band vorgestellten Webseiten wurden entweder für die Aufnahme in die Website webdesignindex.org nominiert, stammen aus den Portfolios preisgekrönter Webdesigner oder sind Entwürfe junger Designer, die mit ihren kreativen Arbeiten auf sich aufmerksam gemacht haben. Bei der Auswahl wurde nicht nur das visuelle Design berücksichtigt, sondern auch die Funktionalität der jeweiligen Webseite und der innovative Einsatz neuer Technologien.

Für jede Website wird die URL angegeben. Die Angaben zu den für Design und Programmierung Verantwortlichen sind nach folgenden Codes sortiert:

Design	D
Code	C
Produktion	P
Agentur	A
Kontaktadresse	M

In der hinteren Umschlagseite befindet sich eine CD-ROM mit allen Webseiten, die in diesem Band vorgestellt wurden; außerdem finden Sie auf dieser CD Film-Previews zu allen Webseiten, die Animationen oder Filmmaterial enthalten. Die CD ermöglicht die Betrachtung aller Webseiten aus diesem Band, ohne dass dazu die jeweilige Seite im Internet aufgerufen werden muss; darüber hinaus dient sie als Archiv, falls die betreffende Website irgendwann nicht mehr im Internet zu sehen sein sollte. Und wenn Sie eine bestimmte Website lieber komplett betrachten wollen, können Sie sie mit Hilfe der auf der CD enthaltenen Links direkt aufrufen.

Vorschläge und Empfehlungen

Pepin Press bringt jedes Jahr eine neue Ausgabe seiner führenden Nachschlagewerke zum Thema Webdesign heraus: **Web Design Index** und **Web Design Index by Content**. Wenn Sie eine Website für unsere zukünftigen Publikationen vorschlagen oder empfehlen möchten, verwenden Sie bitte das entsprechende Formular auf www.webdesignindex.org

The Pepin Press

Weitere Informationen zu den zahlreichen Veröffentlichungen von Pepin Press — in den Bereichen Design, Mode und Popkultur, mit visuellem Referenzmaterial und sofort verwendbaren Bildern für Designer — finden Sie auf unserer Website www.pepinpress.com.

Introduzione

Web Design Index è diventato il punto di riferimento per la ricerca e la catalogazione delle novità nel web design. I siti presentati nelle varie serie sono stati selezionati tra quelli nominati su webdesignindex.org, dal portfolio dei designer che hanno ricevuto di recente premi specifici del settore e i designer emergenti che hanno ricevuto riconoscimenti per il valore innovativo delle loro opere. Il processo di selezione si concentra sul design visivo, ma anche sulla funzionalità e l'uso originale delle nuove tecnologie.

Per ogni sito è indicato l'URL corrispondente. I nomi delle persone che hanno collaborato al design e alla programmazione dei siti sono riportati come segue:

D design
C codificazione
P produzione
A agenzia
M contatti del designer

Il CD-ROM che contiene tutte le pagine web presentate in questo libro si trova nel retrocopertina. Sono incluse delle immagini promozionali di ogni sito che contiene animazioni o filmati. Il CD consente di vedere il design delle pagine web senza accedere a Internet e funge da archivio qualora le pagine venissero tolte dalla rete. Se si preferisce vedere i siti nella loro completezza, il CD contiene hyperlink diretti.

Segnalazioni

Ogni anno The Pepin Press pubblica un'edizione aggiornata dei due punti di riferimento principali per il settore del web design: **Web Design Index** e **Web Design Index by Content**. Se desiderate inviare o segnalare un progetto grafico in particolare, compilate l'apposito modulo sul sito www.webdesignindex.org.

The Pepin Press

Per ulteriori informazioni su The Pepin Press o per ordinare le nostre pubblicazioni dedicate a design, moda, cultura popolare, banca immagini e consultazione grafica, visitate il sito **www.pepinpress.com**.

El **Índice de diseño de páginas web** se ha convertido en la referencia del sector en materia de búsqueda y catalogación de páginas web innovadoras en cuanto a su diseño. Las páginas web ilustradas en esta serie se seleccionan a partir de las nominadas en webdesignindex.org, así como entre los trabajos de los diseñadores premiados recientemente y la obra de nuevos creadores a quienes se ha reconocido recientemente por su diseño innovador. El proceso de selección no se concentra exclusivamente en el diseño, sino también en la funcionalidad y en el uso innovador de nuevas tecnologías.

Se indica la URL de cada sitio que aparece en el libro. El nombre de las personas que han participado en el diseño y la programación de dichos sitios se recoge del modo siguiente:

diseño	D
codificación	C
producción	P
agencia	A
dirección de contacto del diseñador	M

En el interior de la contracubierta se adjunta un CD-ROM con todas las páginas web reproducidas en el libro. Además, se incluyen previsualizaciones de aquellas páginas que contienen animaciones o películas. El CD permite ver el diseño de la página web sin necesidad de conectarse a Internet y sirve como archivo en caso de que las páginas web dejen de estar activas. Si prefiere consultar la web completa, puede acceder a ella mediante los enlaces directos incluidos en el CD.

Propuestas y recomendaciones

Cada año, The Pepin Press publica nuevas ediciones de sus dos libros de referencia en materia de diseño de páginas web: **Web Design Index** y **Web Design Index by Content**. Si desea proponer o recomendar un diseño para que se tenga en cuenta en próximas ediciones, rellene el formulario que figura en: www.webdesignindex.org.

The Pepin Press

Para obtener más información acerca de las numerosas publicaciones de The Pepin Press sobre diseño, moda, cultura popular, referencia visual e imágenes listas para utilizar, visite: **www.pepinpress.com**.

Introdução

O **Catálogo de Web Design** tornou-se o padrão da indústria para acompanhar e catalogar as inovações no mundo do Web Design. Os sites destacados nesta série foram seleccionados a partir dos sites nomeados em webdesignindex.org, dos portefólios de designers que foram laureados recentemente com prémios pelo seu trabalho na Web e ainda do trabalho de novos designers distinguidos pela sua inovação. Além do design, o processo de selecção tem em conta a funcionalidade dos sites e o uso inovador de novas tecnologias.

É indicado o URL de cada sítio na Web presente no livro. Os nomes das pessoas envolvidas na concepção e programação dos sítios na Web são indicados da seguinte forma:

D   design
C   codificação
P   produção
A   agência
M   endereço de contacto do designer

No interior da contracapa, encontrará um CD-ROM com todas as páginas referenciadas neste livro. Estão também incluídas pré-visualizações em vídeo de todos os sites Web que contêm animações ou filmes. O CD permite visualizar o design do site sem ser necessário aceder à Internet e funciona como um arquivo, caso os sites sejam retirados da Internet. Caso prefira ver o site Web na totalidade, pode utilizar as hiperligações existentes no CD para ir directamente para o site.

Propostas e recomendações

Todos os anos, a The Pepin Press publica novas edições de dois livros de referência no âmbito do Web design: **Web Design Index** e **Web Design Index by Content**. Para propor ou recomendar designs à nossa avaliação, aceda ao formulário de propostas em www.webdesignindex.org

The Pepin Press

Para obter mais informações sobre a The Pepin Press ou para efectuar encomendas das nossas obras sobre design, moda, cultura popular, referências visuais e imagens prontas a usar, visite **www.pepinpress.com**

L'**Index de modèles de sites web** est devenu la norme du suivi et du catalogage des innovations en matière de conception Web. Les sites figurant dans cette série sont sélectionnés parmi ceux nominés par le site Web webdesignindex.org, les portefeuilles des concepteurs ayant récemment reçu des prix Web et les œuvres de jeunes concepteurs reconnus pour leurs innovations. Le processus de sélection met l'accent non seulement sur l'aspect visuel, mais également sur la fonctionnalité et l'utilisation novatrice de nouvelles technologies.

L'URL de chaque site est indiquée. Les noms des personnes ayant participé à l'élaboration et à la programmation du site sont classés comme suit :

design	D
programmation	C
production	P
agence	A
adresse du concepteur	M

Un CD-ROM reprenant toutes les pages du livre se trouve en troisième de couverture. Des aperçus vidéo de tous les sites Web contenant des animations ou des séquences sont également inclus. Le CD vous permet de voir le modèle des sites sans connexion à Internet et fonctionne comme des archives permettant la consultation hors ligne des sites Web . Si vous préférez voir l'intégralité du site Web, les liens hypertexte du CD vous y conduisent directement.

Suggestions et recommandations

Chaque année, The Pepin Press publie de nouvelles éditions de ses deux ouvrages de référence en matière de conception virtuelle : **Index de modèles de sites web** et **Index de modèles de sites web par contenu**. Si vous avez des modèles à nous suggérer ou à nous recommander, veuillez remplir le formulaire de suggestion qui se trouve à l'adresse www.webdesignindex.org.

The Pepin Press

Pour en savoir plus sur The Pepin Press ou pour commander un ouvrage parmi notre sélection de publications consacrées au design, à la mode, à la culture pop, aux références visuelles et aux images prêtes à l'emploi, rendez-vous sur notre site Web **www.pepinpress.com**.

Wstęp

Książka **Web Design Index** stała się standardem branżowym w poszukiwaniu i katalogowaniu innowacyjnych projektów stron internetowych. Strony przedstawione w tej części wybrane zostały z tych nominowanych na stronie webdesignindex.org, pochodzą ze zbiorów zdjęć nagrodzonych niedawno projektantów oraz z prac młodych projektantów, którzy otrzymali uznanie za innowacyjne projekty. Podczas procesu selekcji koncentrowano się nie tylko na projektach wizualnych, ale także na funkcjonalności danej strony oraz innowacyjnym zastosowaniu nowych technologii.

Do każdej strony internetowej podawany jest adres URL. Nazwiska osób zaangażowanych w projektowanie i programowanie stron internetowych podawane są następująco:

D   projektowanie
C   kodowanie
P   wykonanie
A   agencja
M   adres email projektanta

Wewnątrz tylnej okładki znajduje się CD-ROM ze wszystkimi stronami internetowymi przedstawionymi w książce. Na płycie znajdują się także zajawki filmowe stron zawierających animacje oraz filmy. Płyta umożliwia Państwu przeglądanie projektów stron internetowych bez połączenia z Internetem oraz ich archiwizowanie w trybie offline. Poprzez kliknięcie hiperłącza na płycie mogą Państwo również oglądać strony internetowe w całości.

Propozycje i rekomendacje

Każdego roku wydawnictwo The Pepin Press publikuje nowe edycje dwóch książek z zakresu projektowania stron internetowych: **Web Design Index** oraz **Web Design Index by Content**. Jeśli chcieliby Państwo przedłożyć lub polecić nam projekt, proszę wypełnić odpowiedni formularz na stronie internetowej www.webdesignindex.org.

Wydawnictwo The Pepin Press

Więcej informacji o licznych publikacjach wydawnictwa The Pepin Press na temat projektowania, mody, kultury, referencji wizualnych oraz gotowych do bezpośredniego użycia obrazów znajdą Państwo na stronie internetowej **www.pepinpress.com**.

Web Design Index (Индекс Веб-Дизайна) стал промышленным стандартом для мониторинга и каталогизации инноваций веб-дизайна. Сайты, фигурирующие в этой серии, выбраны из номинированных на сайте webdesignindex.org, из портфолио дизайнеров, получивших в последние годы премии за веб-дизайн, и из работ новых дизайнеров, заслуживших признание за новационный дизайн. Процесс отбора сосредоточен не только на визуальном дизайне, но и на функциональности и новаторском использовании новых технологий.

Для каждого сайта, приведенного в книге, указывается его адрес (URL). Фамилии людей, принимавших участие в проектировании и создании сайтов, отмечены следующим образом:

дизайн	D
программирование	C
производство	P
агентство	A
контактный адрес дизайнера	M

Компакт-диск, содержащий все страницы этой книги, можно найти на задней сторонке обложки. Для всех сайтов, содержащих анимацию или (видео)фильмы, прилагаются анонсы фильмов. Компакт-диск обеспечивает возможность просматривать дизайн сайта без доступа в Интернет и работает в качестве архива, если веб-сайты просматриваются в автономном режиме. Если предпочитаете просматривать весь веб-сайт, гипертекстовые связи компакт-диска предоставят вам возможность непосредственного просмотра.

Подача на рассмотрение заявок и рекомендации

Каждый год The Pepin Press публикует новые издания книг по веб-дизайну: **Web Design Index** и **Web Design Index by Content**. Если вы желаете подать на рассмотрение заявку или порекомендовать какой-либо дизайн, заполните, пожалуйста, бланк заявки на сайте www.webdesignindex.org.

Издательство The Pepin Press

За дополнительной информацией об основных публикациях издательства The Pepin Press по дизайну, моде, современной культуре, визуальным справочникам и библиотекам высококачественных изображений, готовых к непосредственному использованию, обращайтесь на сайт **www.pepinpress.com**.

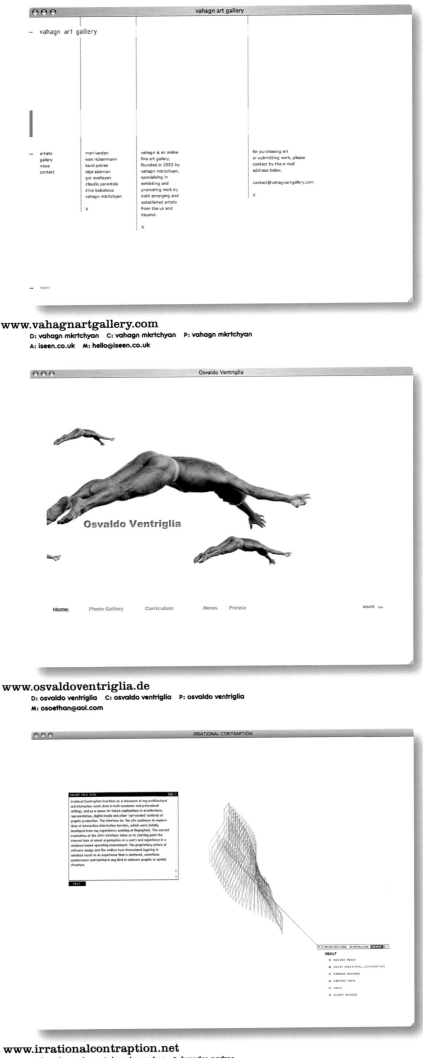

www.vahagnartgallery.com
D: vahagn mkrtchyan   C: vahagn mkrtchyan   P: vahagn mkrtchyan
A: iseen.co.uk   M: hello@iseen.co.uk

www.osvaldoventriglia.de
D: osvaldo ventriglia   C: osvaldo ventriglia   P: osvaldo ventriglia
M: osoethan@aol.com

www.irrationalcontraption.net
D: brandon padron   C: brandon padron   P: brandon padron
M: padron@irrationalcontraption.net

www.antonio-moreno.com

D: antonio moreno   C: antonio moreno   P: am branding
A: am branding   M: mail@antonio-moreno.com

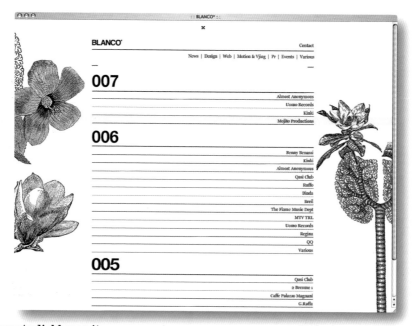

www.studioblanco.it

D: blanco   C: blanco   P: blanco
A: blanco   M: info@studioblanco.it

www.selfselector.com

D: roberto ramos
A: digitalina artworks   M: roberto@digitalina.es

www.fat-man-collective.com
D: david okuniev   C: david okuniev   P: david okuniev
A: fat-man collective   M: david@fat-man-collective.com

www.aaronjasinski.com
D: craig ericson   C: jason keimig
A: section seven   M: jasinski@aaronjasinski.com

www.3dart-online.de/atreides
D: julien minner   C: julien minner   P: julien minner
A: atreides design   M: m2m.studio@t-online.de

www.soop-group.com
D: wai-lian scannell   C: luna raphael
M: admin@soop-group.com

www.wash-design.co.uk
D: andy walmsley, tom kidd   C: dan shaw   P: wash
A: wash design   M: andy@wash-design.co.uk

www.meniconpremio.com
D: estefanía pérez huerga
M: www.ra-marketing.com

22

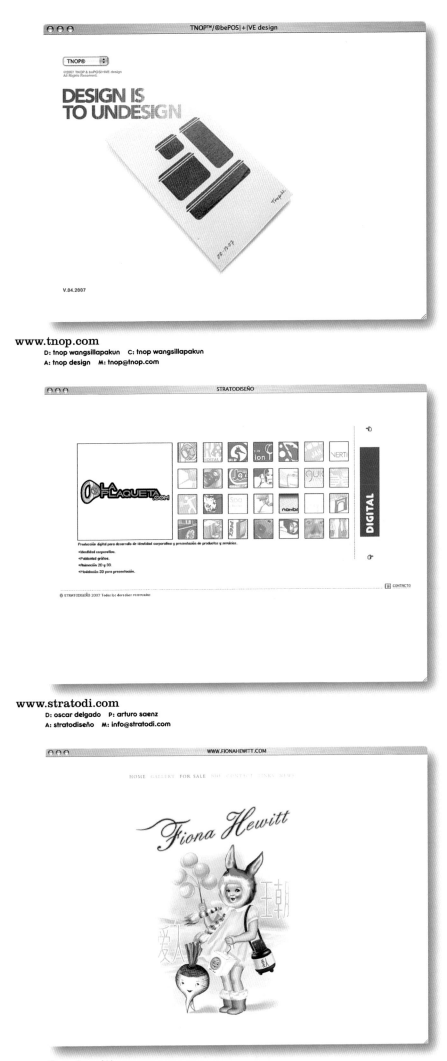

www.tnop.com
D: tnop wangsillapakun   C: tnop wangsillapakun
A: tnop design   M: tnop@tnop.com

www.stratodi.com
D: oscar delgado   P: arturo saenz
A: stratodiseño   M: info@stratodi.com

www.fionahewitt.com
D: fiona hewitt   C: andrew tainton   P: fiona hewitt
A: fiona hewitt ltd.   M: fiona@fionahewitt.com

l–aleph
l'ospite tiranno

guarda,
installazione per l'Ospite Tiranno. 2007 (carte dipinte, specchio)
Presso il palazzo Tiranni-Castracane a Cagli, otto artisti cercano di creare il giusto rapporto tra spazio e identità personale. La scelta delle stanze dove ospitare le installazioni per me è caduta in tutta la sua bellezza, lo stucco del soffitto eseguito dal Brandani alla fine del '500. Impegnativo e fuorviante, ma bello. La necessità di mostrare tale bellezza mi porta a indicare arbitrariamente la presenza del capolavoro forzando la visione verso l'alto (con l'ausilio di un vecchio specchio) andando a perimetrare il luogo delle visione con una serie di dipinti su carta posti come sacerdoti che vigliano e chiudono la concentrazione verso l'alto, lasciando libero solo il passaggio da una stanza all'altra, trasformando quest'ultima in una sorta di palcoscenico, piazza teatrale.

aptico

aptico,
personale presso l'Ex Pescheria, Cesena (FC), 2005
Primo tentativo di elaborare l'idea che sta a monte del termine "aptico" (il testo allegato cerca di introdurre uno dei significati applicati) in forma di esposizione-installazione, presso l'Ex Pescheria di Cesena grande ed evasiva.

"...Qualsiasi tipo di percezione sensoriale è in rapporto con lo spazio circostante. La percezione dello spazio visivo è profondamente diversa da quella dello spazio aptico. Lo spazio visivo è, per il soggetto fermo in un punto, pieno di immagini; nella stessa situazione, lo spazio puramente aptico è vuoto. Infatti, in posizione di assoluta immobilità, magari prolungato nel tempo, lo spazio diviene pressoché impercettibile. In questa situazione, non si ha quasi la sensazione di sé e di fuori di sé. Qualora il corpo si metta in movimento, si ha la percezione di una massa di spazio che non è ancora strutturata, ma che comincia a differenziarsi dal corpo stesso, di cui il soggetto prende coscienza, attraverso la percezione di uno spazio al di fuori di sé. Si viene a determinare, così, la percezione dell'io corporeo. Ma solo quando il soggetto prende in mano un oggetto, percepisce sé come essere in contrapposizione ad esso. Lo spazio attorno a lui e all'oggetto si può suddividere in spazio vicino e lontano, ma mentre la percezione dello spazio vicino è possibile a tutti, vedenti e non, quella dello spazio lontano si manifesta prevalentemente nei vedenti e nei ciechi divenuti tali a tarda età; questi, attraverso la visualizzazione interiore, suppliscono alla mancanza del dato percettivo visivo immediato. In tal modo, però, non si ha la percezione dello spazio aptico, ma la trasposizione dello spazio visivo su quello aptico..."

da Genesi e struttura delle forme tattili web site www.ciad.it/invito/braille/html/ml1.html

dinamismo di un cane al guinzaglio

lo spettacolo, i video.
La piccola esperienza spesa per la creazione e messa in opera dello spettacolo Dinamismo di un cane al guinzaglio mi ha permesso di scoprire la particolare bellezza e fatica di lavorare per il teatro, dentro il teatro. Nata dal lavoro sinergico di un coreografo, un compositore di musica contemporanea e un artista visivo che, insieme ai danzatori cercano di mettere in piedi un sogno (quello dei futuristi) evitando, però, l'ovvia ricaduta citazionista o da avanspettacolo.

cadenza

www.l-aleph.it
D: gian luca proietti   P: gian luca proietti
A: cinabro   M: info@cinabro.it

www.project-mayhem.be
D: pascal liénard   C: pascal liénard   P: pascal liénard
A: pascal liénard   M: info@pascallienard.com

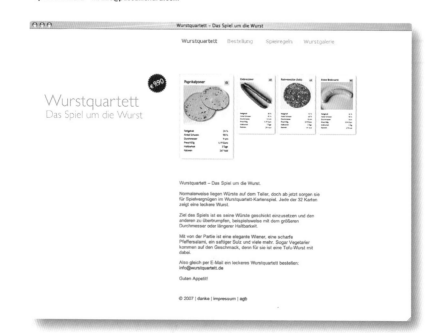

Wurstquartett – Das Spiel um die Wurst.

Normalerweise liegen Würste auf dem Teller, doch ab jetzt sorgen sie für Spielvergnügen im Wurstquartett-Kartenspiel. Jede der 32 Karten zeigt eine leckere Wurst.

Ziel des Spiels ist es seine Würste geschickt einzusetzen und den anderen zu übertrumpfen, beispielsweise mit dem größeren Durchmesser oder längerer Haltbarkeit.

Mit von der Partie ist eine elegante Wiener, eine scharfe Pfeffersalami, ein saftiger Sulz und viele mehr. Sogar Vegetarier kommen auf den Geschmack, denn für sie ist eine Tofu-Wurst mit dabei.

Also gleich per E-Mail ein leckeres Wurstquartett bestellen: info@wurstquartett.de

Guten Appetit!

© 2007 | danke | impressum | agb

www.wurstquartett.de
D: mareike leder   C: mareike leder   P: gerald meilicke
A: www.wurstquartett.de   M: info@wurstquartett.de

www.lechic.biz

D: serialcut   C: serialcut   P: serialcut
A: serialcut   M: rebeka.rbk@gmail.com

www.vectorfabrik.com

D: patrick padeau   C: patrick padeau   P: patrick padeau
A: vectorfabrik   M: patrick@vectorfabrik.com

www.gardens-co.com

D: wilson tang   C: wilson tang
A: gardens&co   M: wilson@gardens-co.com

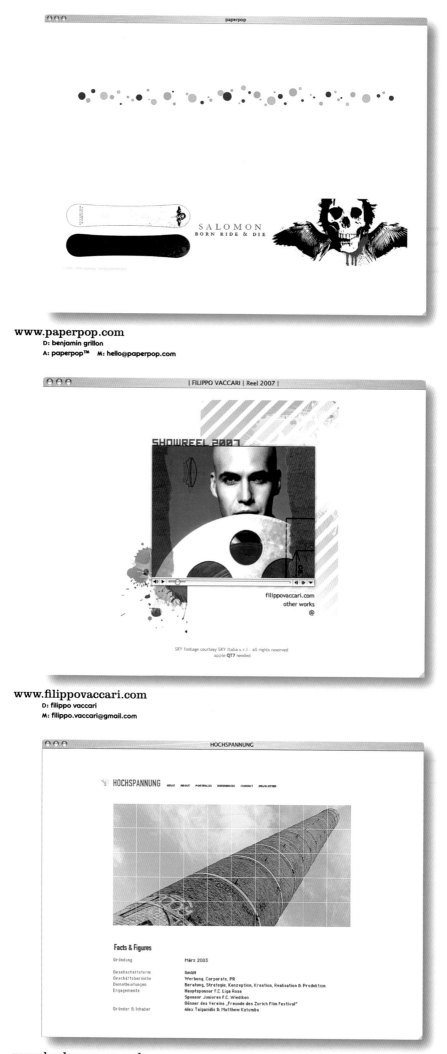

www.paperpop.com
D: benjamin grillon
A: paperpop™   M: hello@paperpop.com

www.filippovaccari.com
D: filippo vaccari
M: filippo.vaccari@gmail.com

www.hochspannung.ch
D: matthew katumba, alex taiganidis, mario thomas   C: group94
A: hochspannung gmbh, zurich   M: taiganidis@hochspannung.ch

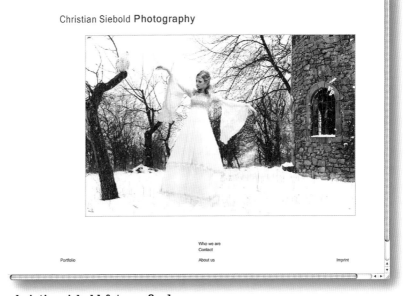

www.christiansiebold-fotografie.de
D: christian siebold   C: christian siebold   P: christian siebold
A: christian siebold photography   M: mail@christiansiebold.de

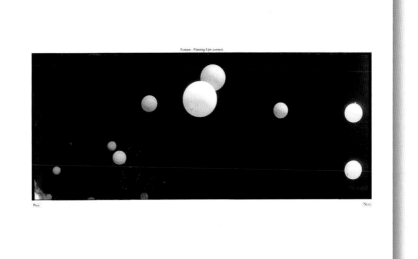

www.panoramicity.com
D: michele lugaresi   C: michele lugaresi   P: michele lugaresi
A: maikid   M: michele@lugaresi.com

www.ninafotka.com
D: andrej čilić   C: andrej čilić
M: cilic.design@gmail.com

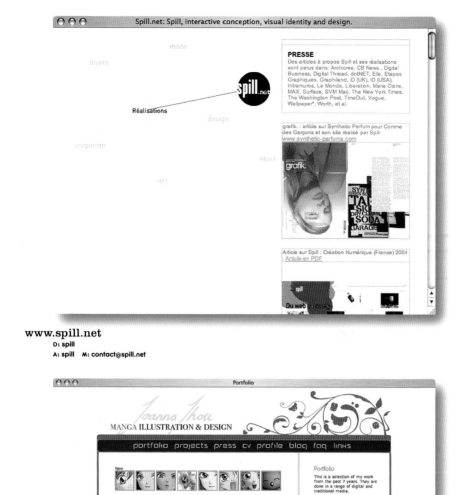

www.spill.net
D: spill
A: spill   M: contact@spill.net

www.chocolatepixels.com
D: joanna zhou
M: joannazhou1@gmail.com

www.waldmann-weinold.de
D: marion waldmann, felix weinold   C: brigitte binder
A: waldmann & weinold, kommunikationsdesign   M: info@waldmann-weinold.de

www.blueprint-studios.com
D: brendan dawes, suzie webb
A: magnetic north   M: tim@blueprint-studios.com

www.racecar.no
D: noon   C: noon
A: noon   M: soon@noon.no

www.mktvirtual.com.br
D: ludmilla rossi   C: mauricio matias
A: mkt virtual   M: ludmilla@mktvirtual.com.br

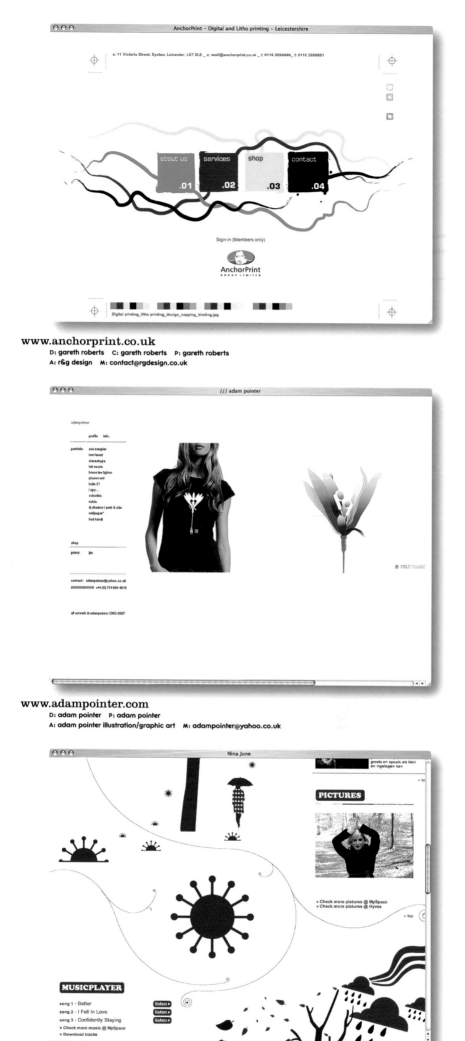

www.anchorprint.co.uk
D: gareth roberts   C: gareth roberts   P: gareth roberts
A: r&g design   M: contact@rgdesign.co.uk

www.adampointer.com
D: adam pointer   P: adam pointer
A: adam pointer illustration/graphic art   M: adampointer@yahoo.co.uk

www.ninajune.com
D: tim schellekens   C: giel wijgergangs   P: sander crombach
A: studio jan koek   M: info@studiojankoek.nl

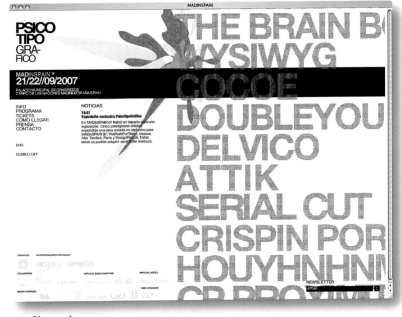

www.madinspain.com
D: abel martínez   C: manuel álvarez
M: info@madinspain.com

www.atalier.com
D: ata "toast" bozaci, amanda beck   C: remy burger   P: remy burger
A: atalier gmbh - visual entertainment   M: info@atalier.com

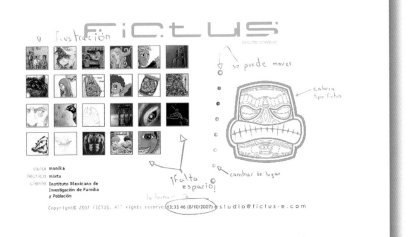

www.fictus-e.com
D: roman medina   C: roman medina
A: fictus estudio   M: estudio@fictus-e.com

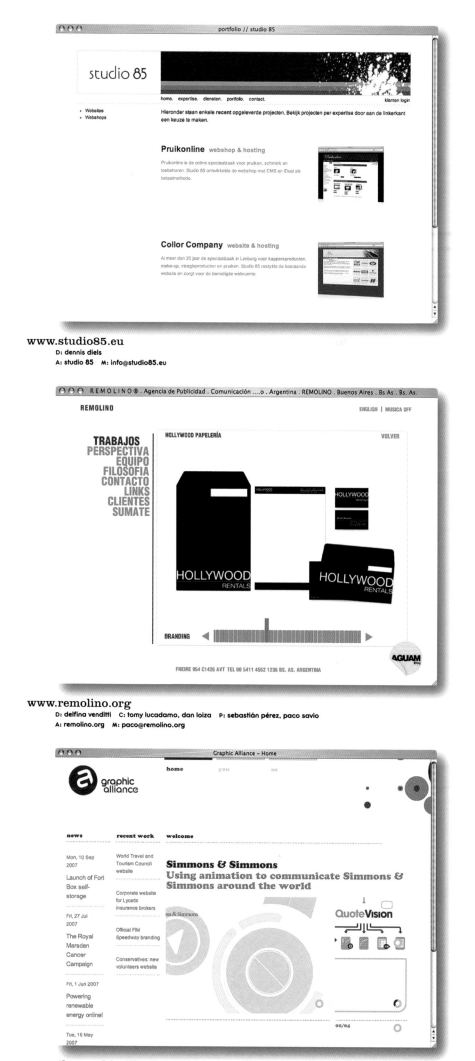

www.studio85.eu

D: dennis diels

A: studio 85   M: info@studio85.eu

www.remolino.org

D: delfina venditti   C: tomy lucadamo, dan loiza   P: sebastián pérez, paco savio

A: remolino.org   M: paco@remolino.org

www.thegraphicalliance.com

D: stuart bowler, jonathon shanks, simon roberts   C: andrew roberts   P: stuart bowler

A: graphic alliance   M: stuart@graphicalliance.co.uk

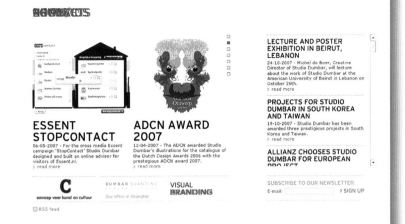

www.studiodumbar.com
D: studio dumbar   C: studio dumbar   P: studio dumbar
A: studio dumbar   M: info@studiodumbar.com

www.mtbcycletech.com
D: g.gasser, m.ziska   C: u.scheidegger   P: fastforward.ch
A: id-k kommunikationsdesign   M: www.id-k.com

mottoform / freeform

mottoform

ABOUT
PRODUCTS
PROJECTS
FREEFORM
doors
eat
random
CONTACT

Taking inspiration from the everyday,
we look at how people live:

eat
sleep
play
connect
interact

FREEFORM

As a company, Mottoform
is fluid and adaptable.

Taking inspiration from
the everyday, we look at
how people live: eat,
sleep, play, connect,
interact.

We're interested in
bringing a sense of
meaning to the ordinary
things we do. We identify
emerging trends, what
people need and desire,
and like to create new
products for new markets.

www.mottoform.com
D: liisa salonen, nina bianchi, elizabeth salonen   C: alex braidwood   P: liisa salonen
A: elevator O1:O2 ltd.   M: www.mottoform.com

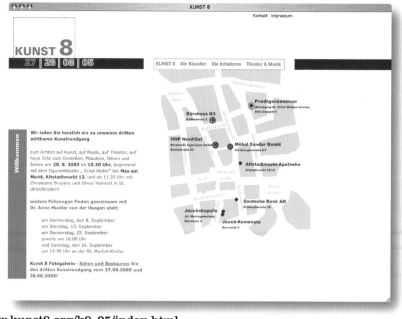

www.kunst8.org/k8_05/index.html

D: saskia pierschek
A: iconnewmedia   M: saskia.pierschek@iconnewmedia.de

www.svidesign.com

D: sasha vidakovic   C: maxim bugarin, iweb   P: sasha vidakovic
A: svidesign   M: sasha@svidesign.com

www.digitalbaba.com

D: filippo montanelli   C: filippo montanelli   P: filippo montanelli
A: digitalbaba design   M: art@digitalbaba.com

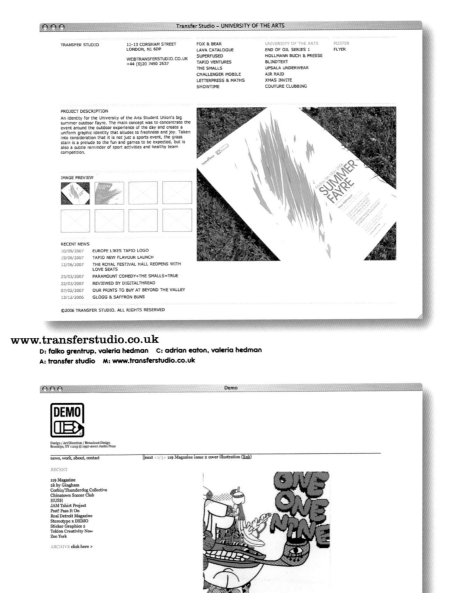

TRANSFER STUDIO

11-13 CORSHAM STREET
LONDON, N1 6DP
WE@TRANSFERSTUDIO.CO.UK
+44 (0)20 7490 2637

FOX & BEAR
LAVA CATALOGUE
SUPERFUSED
TAPIO VENTURES
THE SMALLS
CHALLENGER MOBILE
LETTERPRESS & MATHS
SHOWTIME

UNIVERSITY OF THE ARTS
END OF OIL SERIES 1
HOLLMANN BUCH & PRESSE
BLINDTEXT
UPSALA UNDERWEAR
AIR RAID
XMAS INVITE
COUTURE CLUBBING

POSTER
FLYER

PROJECT DESCRIPTION
An identity for the University of the Arts Student Union's big summer outdoor fayre. The main concept was to concentrate the event around the outdoor experience of the day and create a uniform graphic identity that alludes to freshness and joy. Taken into consideration that it is not just a sports event, the grass stain is a prelude to the fun and games to be expected, but is also a subtle reminder of sport activities and healthy team competition.

IMAGE PREVIEW

RECENT NEWS
10/09/2007 EUROPE LIKES TAPIO LOGO
19/06/2007 TAPIO NEW FLAVOUR LAUNCH
12/06/2007 THE ROYAL FESTIVAL HALL REOPENS WITH LOVE SEATS
23/03/2007 PARAMOUNT COMEDY+THE SMALLS=TRUE
22/03/2007 REVIEWED BY DIGITALTHREAD
07/02/2007 OUR PRINTS TO BUY AT BEYOND THE VALLEY
13/12/2006 GLÖGG & SAFFRON BUNS

www.transferstudio.co.uk
D: falko grentrup, valeria hedman   C: adrian eaton, valeria hedman
A: transfer studio   M: www.transferstudio.co.uk

DEMO

Design / Art Direction / Broadcast Design
Brooklyn, NY 11215 © 1997-2007 Justin Fines

news, work, about, contact

||next < 1/3 > 119 Magazine issue 2 cover illustration (link)

RECENT

119 Magazine
2k by Gingham
Corbis/Thunderdog Collective
Chinatown Soccer Club
HUSH
JAM Tshirt Project
Past! Pass It On
Real Detroit Magazine
Stereotype x DEMO
Sticker Graphics 2
Tokion Creativity Now
Zoo York

ARCHIVE click here >

www.demo-design.com
D: justin fines   C: justin fines
A: demo   M: justin@demo-design.com

dunun   +33 6 37 88 95 15
           email@dunun.com

We design and develop high quality
web sites and interactive media.

+ dunun version 2002

sion

samsung k3

airtist

virtuoz

unik

innovative

kelamali

onsitechicago

benjiben

parishome

samuel vieillard

ten

www.dunun.com
D: micael reynaud   C: micael reynaud   P: micael reynaud
A: dunun   M: webdesignindex@dunun.com

www.studiopoint.hr

D: alen matovina   C: alen matovina   P: alen matovina
A: studio point   M: lena@studiopoint.hr

www.noventaynueve.com

D: carlos ulloa   C: carlos ulloa   P: carlos ulloa
A: carlosulloa.com   M: info@carlosulloa.com

www.max-more.com.tw

D: martin lee   C: tom
A: maxmore design   M: martin@max-more.com.tw

www.pockoville.com/main.html
D: javier nieto   C: gonzalo   P: acrilik
A: pocko   M: agency@pocko.com

www.atedadesign.com
D: ermal turkesi   C: ermal turkesi
A: ateda llc   M: design@ateda.com

www.typisk.nu
D: kasper riisholt, nanna skytte   C: pelle kroegholt, sille bjarnhof
A: typisk   M: info@typisk.nu

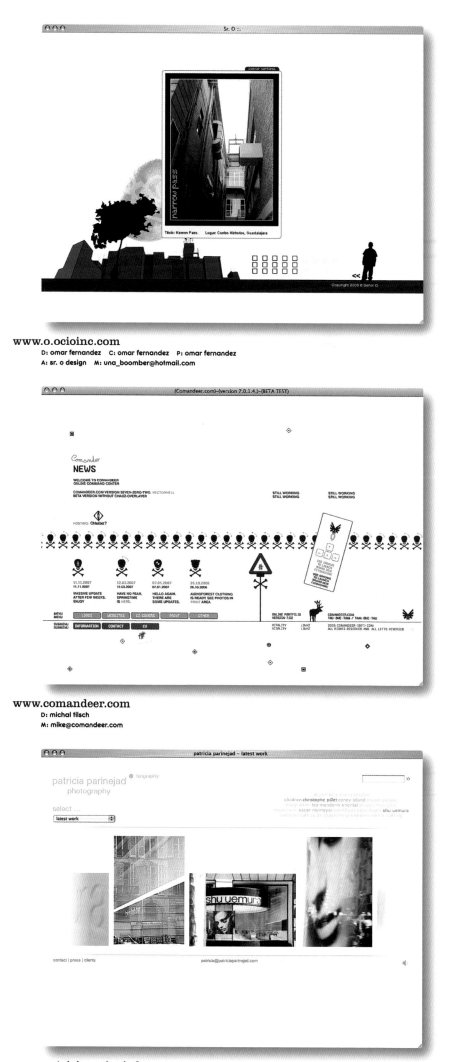

www.o.ocioinc.com
D: omar fernandez   C: omar fernandez   P: omar fernandez
A: sr. o design   M: una_boomber@hotmail.com

www.comandeer.com
D: michal tilsch
M: mike@comandeer.com

www.patriciaparinejad.com
D: thierry houillon   P: michael montmoril
A: vhox.com   M: contact@vhox.com

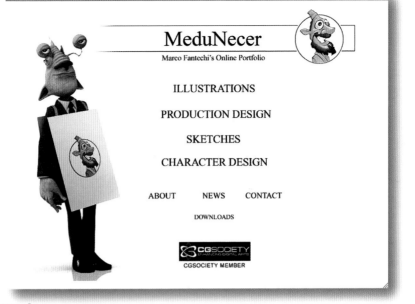

www.medunecer.com

D: marco fantechi   C: marco fantechi   P: marco fantechi
A: medunecer   M: info@medunecer.com

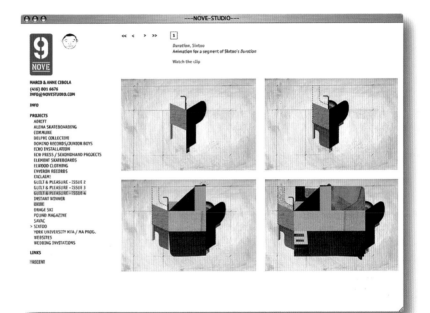

www.novestudio.com

D: anne cibola   C: marco cibola
A: nove studio   M: info@novestudio.com

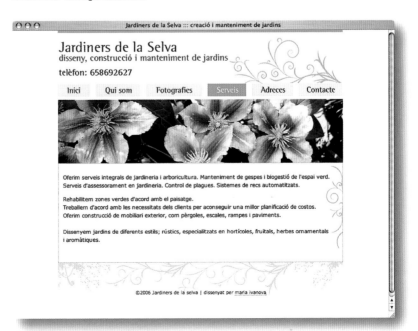

www.jardinersdelaselva.com

D: maria ivanova   C: maria ivanova   P: maria ivanova
A: maria ivanova   M: www.maria-ivanova.com

www.miguelcaetano.com
D: marta faustino   C: marta faustino   P: marta faustino
A: marta faustino   M: www.martafaustino.com

www.davefahreza.com
D: dave fahreza
M: dkezz10@gmail.com

www.computernotdienst-leipzig.de
D: christina kandlhofer   C: tom steinbeck, christina kandlhofer   P: christina kandlhofer
A: kashi_design   M: www.kashi.at

www.walnuthilldesign.com
D: tim atkins   C: tim atkins
A: walnut hill design   M: info@walnuthilldesign.com

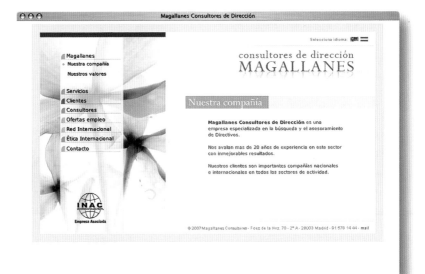

www.magallanesconsultores.com
D: daniel eguíluz hernández   C: eva giménez   P: carlos aldama
A: dipro   M: daniel.eguiluz@dipro.es

www.asicsdesigncompetition.com
D: ruud hendrikx, tom konings, chester griët   C: tom konings   P: ruud hendrikx
A: formidastic   M: ruud@formidastic.com

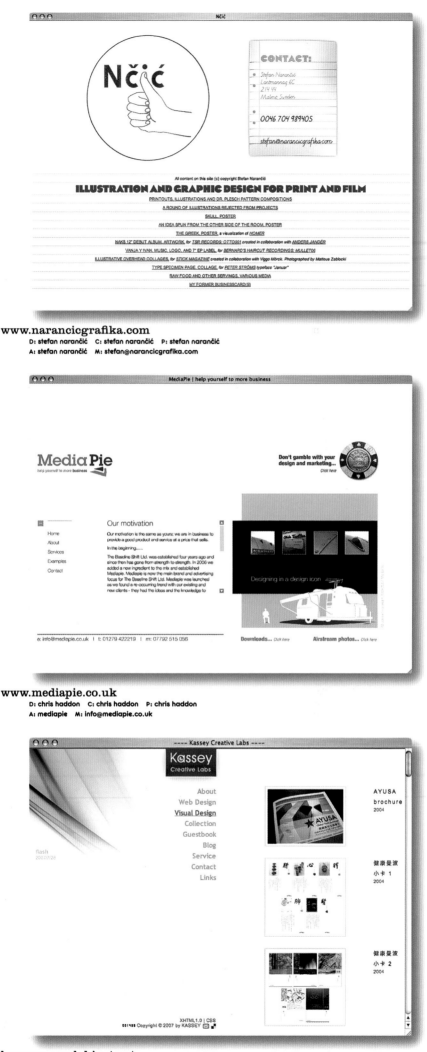

www.narancicgrafika.com
D: stefan narančić   C: stefan narančić   P: stefan narančić
A: stefan narančić   M: stefan@narancicgrafika.com

www.mediapie.co.uk
D: chris haddon   C: chris haddon   P: chris haddon
A: mediapie   M: info@mediapie.co.uk

kassey.myweb.hinet.net
D: kassey   C: kassey   P: kassey
A: kasseyworks   M: kasseyworks@gmail.com

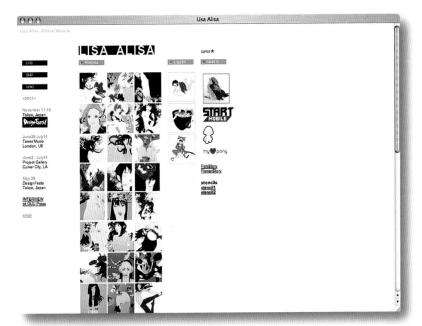

www.lisa-alisa.com
D: lisa alisa   C: lisa alisa   P: lisa alisa
M: summerfinch@gmail.com

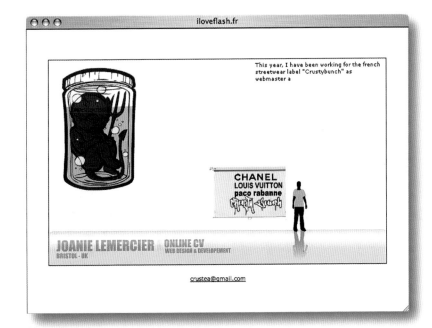

www.iloveflash.fr
D: joanie lemercier   C: joanie lemercier   P: joanie lemercier
A: cremefraiche   M: crustea@free.fr

www.nssgraphica.com
D: munehiro machida
A: nssgraphica   M: info@nssgraphica.com

www.huidilauhoff.de
D: scholz   C: scholz   P: scholz
A: scholz   M: contact@huidilauhoff.de

www.studiojankoek.nl
D: sander crombach   C: sander crombach   P: tim schellekens
A: studio jan koek   M: info@studiojankoek.nl

splinesystem.free.fr
D: savoia   C: savoia   P: savoia
A: splinesystem   M: splinesystem@free.fr

www.contreforme.ch
D: noémie oulevay   C: sam rossetti   P: contreforme
A: contreforme   M: info@contreforme.ch

www.republik.ca
D: marcin leskiewicz, carl dionne   C: pixelwarehouse
A: republik   M: info@republik.ca

www.eyegix.com
D: daniel bretzmann   C: daniel bretzmann   P: daniel bretzmann
A: eyegix™   M: input@eyegix.com

numiko.com
D: stuart jacklin   C: jaron ghani   P: david eccles
A: numiko   M: dave@numiko.com

www.redshows.net
D: kikoh shimula   C: kikoh shimula   P: kikoh shimula
A: studio cage   M: email@studiocage.com

www.servatius-rechtsanwaelte.de
D: dirk heinemann   C: henning lehfeldt   P: anke rippert
A: nordisch.com   M: heinemann@nordisch.com

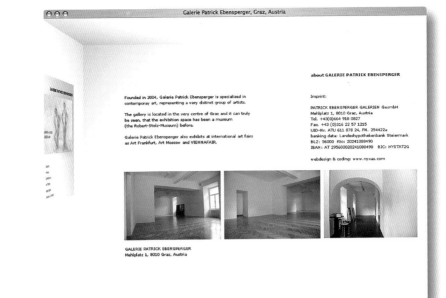

Galerie Patrick Ebensperger, Graz, Austria

about GALERIE PATRICK EBENSPERGER

Founded in 2004, Galerie Patrick Ebensperger is specialized in contemporay art, representing a very distinct group of artists.

The gallery is located in the very centre of Graz and it can truly be seen, that the exhibition space has been a museum (the Robert-Stolz-Museum) before.

Galerie Patrick Ebensperger also exhibits at international art fairs as Art Frankfurt, Art Moscow and VIENNAFAIR.

Imprint:

PATRICK EBENSPERGER GALERIEN GesmbH
Mehlplatz 1, 8010 Graz, Austria
Tel. +43(0)664 918 0827
Fax. +43 (0)316 22 57 1215
UID-Nr. ATU 611 878 24, FN. 254422a
banking data: Landeshypothekenbank Steiermark
BLZ: 56000 Kto: 20241088490
IBAN: AT 295600020241088490 BIC: HYSTAT2G

webdesign & coding: www.nyxas.com

GALERIE PATRICK EBENSPERGER
Mehlplatz 1, 8010 Graz, Austria

www.ebensperger.net
D: alexander baldele   C: katja ratschiller   P: markus angerer
A: nyxas   M: office@nyxas.com

RICHARD FENWICK

Some Recent Films:

The Box - 8 min, Colour, 16mm

Festivals & Awards

+ Curtocircuíto, International Short Film Festival, Santiago de Compostela, 2007
+ CineGlobe International Short Film Festival, Geneva 2007
+ Finalist, 16th Kodak Film Showcase, London 2007
+ Shortlisted, Rushes Soho Shorts, London 2007
+ Dokufest, Prizren, Kosovo, 2007
+ Impakt, Utrecht, Netherlands 2007
+ 4th Halloween Film Festival, London 2007
+ NLFF, Newcastle 2006
+ RESFEST International tour 2006

Love Letter - 8 min, Colour, 16mm

Festivals & Awards

+ Latitude, South East England 2007
+ Britspotting, Berlin 2007
+ Very Short Movies Film Festival, LA 2007
+ 4th Halloween Film Festival, London 2007
+ NLFF, Newcastle 2006
+ 51st Cork Film Festival, Ireland 2006

Some Recent Animations:

What We've Found Out About Stem Cells - 13 min, Colour, Digital

Festivals & Awards

+ Mecal International Short Film Festival, Barcelona 2007
+ Runner Up, Rushes Soho Shorts, London 2007
+ 3rd Digital Barcelona Film Festival 2007
+ Silver, Rose Design Awards, Manchester 2006, for best DVD
+ RESFEST International tour 2006
+ onedotzero_10, International tour 2006
+ AV06 Festival, North East England 2006

USERGUIDES®
30 min, Colour, Digital

Festivals & Awards

+ onedotzero_11, International tour 2007
+ NLFF, Newcastle 2007

Safety Procedures

Contact Richard:

info@richardfenwick.com

Representation:

Film & Television:

For theatrical feature, television and cable representation please contact Melinda Jason at her management company:
Conspiracy, 9864 National Boulevard #181, Los Angeles, California 90034 (310) 287-1723.
melinda@conspiracymedia.net

Sales & Distribution:

Short Films:

For sales, distribution and exhibition enquiries please contact: onedotzero +44 (0)207 729 0072
ben@onedotzero.com

For the short film Love Letter - contact:
Shorts International +44 (0)207 734 2277
simon@britshorts.com

Some Recent Press:

+ 4Talent interview
+ Director's Notes: What We've Found Out About Stem Cells
+ Screen International: The UK Stars of Tomorrow, 2007
+ RES Magazine: Richard Fenwick's fractured filmmaking
+ Creative Review: Artificial Worlds V3.0, First Sight
+ Guardian Guide/Observer Review: If you see one thing... AV Festival 06
+ Hotdog Magazine: Going Underground: Cherry

www.richardfenwick.com
D: richard fenwick   C: richard fenwick   P: richard fenwick
A: richard fenwick   M: info@richardfenwick.com

TOCA ME

get your early bird ticket!

TOCA ME PRESENTS
**DESIGN CONFERENCE 08
SATURDAY 23/02/08
MUNICH, GERMANY**

DESIGN STUDIO

09/2007
we have finally relaunched our design studio website with projects from print, web, event and virtual worlds.

08/2007
the microsite for dsf's campaign and raffle 'meine zweite' just went online.

DESIGN EVENTS

09/2007
TOCA ME design conference 08 in munich on 23/02/2008 now online - get your ticket now!

09/2007
TOCA ME and LOUNGE SEVENTY-TWO™ present BEYOND SURFACE DESIGN CONTEST - join in!

DESIGN COMMUNITY

09/2007
new artists featured in the watch me section: niko stumpo and mate steinfort.

07/2007
our latest design heroes are stefan rizler and jasmine l. read the interview in our blog.

design blog // contact // newsletter // press /////////// legal notice / impressum   (mt)

www.toca-me.com
D: thorsten iberl, nina schmid   C: ronald iberl, thorsten iberl   P: toca me
A: toca me   M: info@toca-me.com

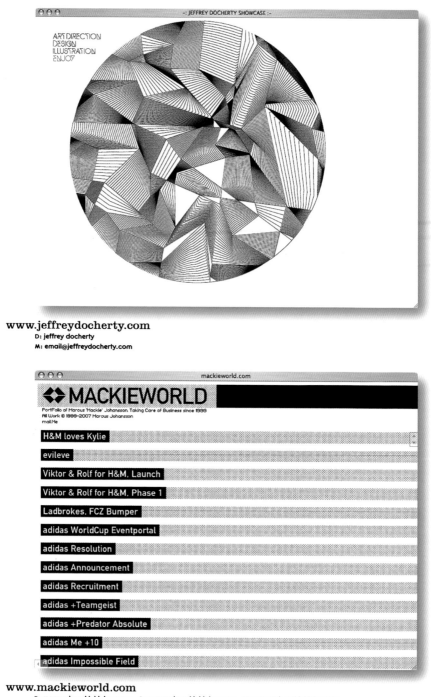

ART DIRECTION
DESIGN
ILLUSTRATION
ENJOY

-:- JEFFREY DOCHERTY SHOWCASE :-

www.jeffreydocherty.com
D: jeffrey docherty
M: email@jeffreydocherty.com

mackieworld.com

◆ MACKIEWORLD
Portfolio of Marcus 'Mackie' Johansson. Taking Care of Business since 1999
All Work © 1999-2007 Marcus Johansson
mail.Me

H&M loves Kylie

evileve

Viktor & Rolf for H&M, Launch

Viktor & Rolf for H&M, Phase 1

Ladbrokes, FCZ Bumper

adidas WorldCup Eventportal

adidas Resolution

adidas Announcement

adidas Recruitment

adidas +Teamgeist

adidas +Predator Absolute

adidas Me +10

adidas Impossible Field

www.mackieworld.com
D: marcus 'mackie' johansson   C: marcus 'mackie' johansson   P: marcus 'mackie' johansson
M: word@mackieworld.com

Anton Sword

| home | **info & press** | news & shows | contact & buy | play/stop ◀))

Anton Sword

One day when he was a child in New York City, Anton put his ear against a speaker in a dark apartment on the west side and went into a trance. He had a long dream. When he woke up twenty years later his heart was permanently broken, but in a good way. Trying to make a movie out of the turbulence in his mind, he found himself writing songs instead. Some people compare his songs to Roxy Music's, some to John Lennon's, and some to a session of great sex during psychoanalysis.

Anton decided to make some CDs to get it all out of his system, and then go back to sleep. The first CD, **A Sentimental Education**, is now available at CDBaby and many record stores across the United States. And of course, it is available at live shows. **Lush, dreamy, mesmerizing, groovy, catchy,** and **gorgeous** are some of the words New Yorkes and Berliners have used to describe it.

From the first line--"got the wrong-sized leash out for your heart" (the brooding of a man wandering a library of moods somewhere "where the midnight's backbone doubles back") --to the last line, "coming down to earth in the ship of jewels,"-- **A Sentimental Education** leads from one song to the next like chapters of a novel. It's a story that follows a winding thread sewing together the open day with the darker chambers of the heart, emerging at the end into a melancholy but hopeful cadence and the long slow tailoff of a slightly sad sexual afterglow fading into blackness...

Sometimes, as you can see from the preceding paragraph, Anton takes himself a little too seriously, but his

www.antonsword.com
D: andrea fröhner   C: aaston brooks
M: afroehn@gmx.de

48

www.sergiosotomayor.com
D: sergio sotomayor   C: sergio sotomayor   P: sergio sotomayor
A: sergio sotomayor   M: info@sergiosotomayor.com

www.dotkitelab.eu
D: thomas mylonas, matteo modica   C: paulo campos   P: dot kite
A: dot kite   M: info@dotkitelab.eu

www.scienceunderfire.com
D: david löhr
M: contact@scienceunderfire.com

www.tenmetal.com

D: paul wagner   C: paul wagner   P: paul wagner

A: tenmetal design   M: desk@tenmetal.com

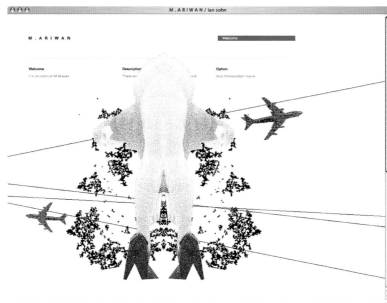

www.kioskue.com

D: demian sohn (sohn haang seok)   C: demian sohn   P: demian sohn

A: alice ct.   M: m.ariwan@kioskue.com

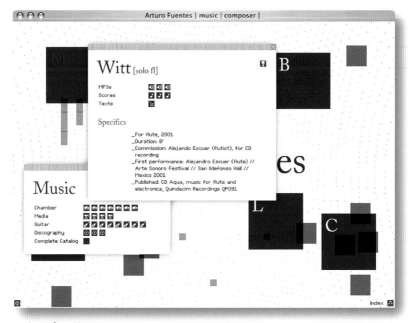

www.arturofuentes.com

D: rainer fabrizi   C: rainer fabrizi   P: transporter concept.print.web.

A: transporter concept.print.web.   M: fabrizi@transporter.at

www.hunterandgatti.com
D: hunter and gatti   C: hunter and gatti   P: hunter and gatti
A: hunter and gatti   M: info@hunterandgatti.com

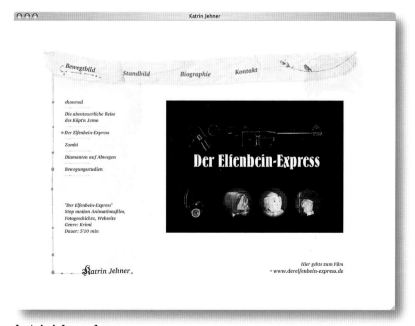

www.salzigdesign.com
D: stephan landschütz   C: sebastian assenheimer
A: salzigdesign   M: info@salzigdesign.com

www.katrinjehner.de
D: katrin jehner   C: katrin jehner
M: katjeh@gmx.de

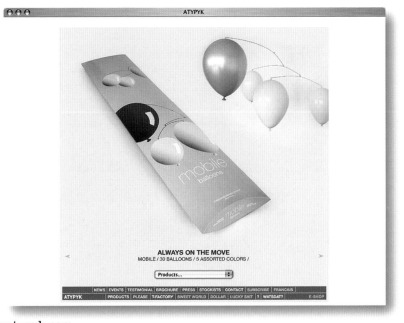

www.luceper.com
D: simona carbotta   C: simona carbotta   P: roberto enrietti
A: ege.comunicazione   M: www.egecomunicazione.it

www.atypyk.com
D: jean sébastien ides   C: jean sébastien ides
A: atypyk   M: ivan@atypyk.com

www.loyalstudios.com
D: loyal chow   C: loyal chow   P: loyal chow
A: loyal studios   M: loyal@loyalstudios.com

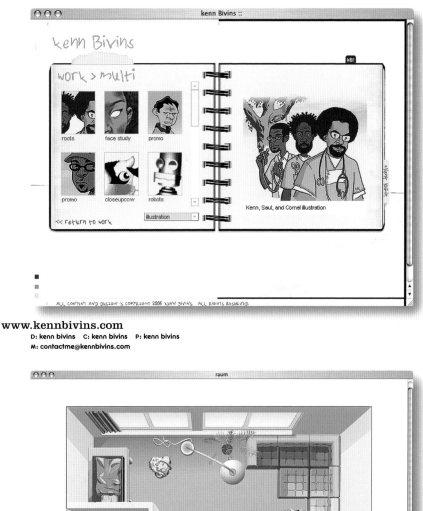

www.kennbivins.com
D: kenn bivins   C: kenn bivins   P: kenn bivins
M: contactme@kennbivins.com

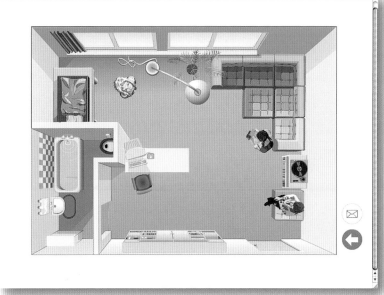

www.ankebauer.de
D: anke bauer   C: martin haak, anke bauer   P: anke bauer
A: anke bauer   M: anke@ankebauer.de

www.lineamediterranea.it
D: gian nicola maestro   P: lucio carli
A: www.gnm.it   M: www.gnm.it

www.amodesign.net
D: bruno galrito   C: renato soares   P: antónio amaro
A: amodesign, comunicação gráfica e digital   M: bruno@amodesign.net

www.carstenmell.com
D: carsten mell   C: visor 3000   P: carsten mell
M: info@carstenmell.com

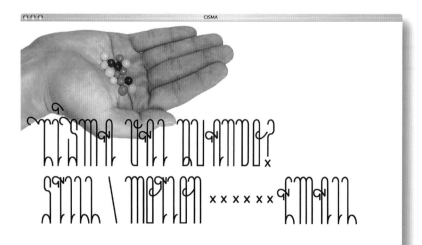

www.cisma.com.br
D: denis kamioka   C: denis kamioka   P: denis kamioka
A: cisma   M: muitoprazer@cisma.com.br

www.loopland.net
D: allan sanders   C: allan sanders
M: allan@loopland.net

www.jtillustration.com
D: james turner   C: daniel sadowski
A: james turner illustration   M: james@jtillustration.com

www.cultivatorads.com
D: ian coyle   C: ian coyle
A: superheroes   M: ian@superhero.es

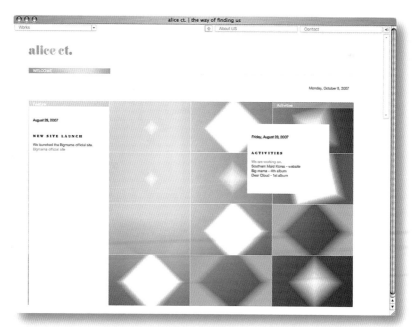

www.alicect.com
D: demian sohn (sohn haang seok)   C: demian sohn   P: demian sohn
A: alice ct.   M: m.ariwan@alicect.com

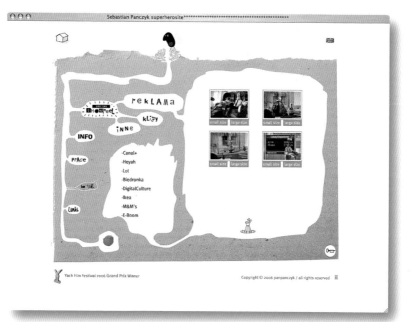

www.panpanczyk.com
D: sebastian panczyk   C: marek mielnicki   P: sebastian panczyk
A: dobro sebastian panczyk   M: dobro4@wp.pl

www.beautifulfreak.be
D: frederik vanderfaeillie   C: gaëtan lafaut   P: beautiful freak
A: chilli design   M: www.chilli.be

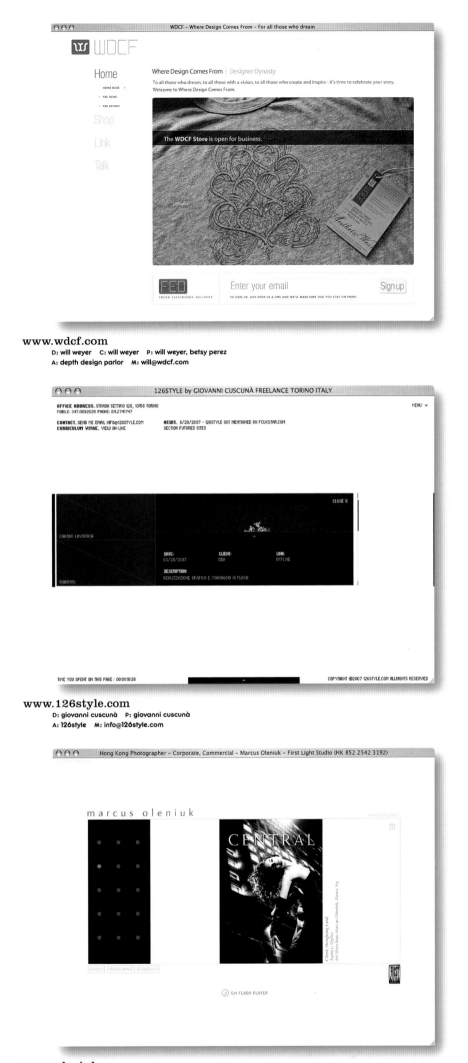

www.wdcf.com

D: will weyer   C: will weyer   P: will weyer, betsy perez
A: depth design parlor   M: will@wdcf.com

www.126style.com

D: giovanni cuscunà   P: giovanni cuscunà
A: 126style   M: info@126style.com

www.oleniuk.com

D: dharmistha bradley, ketan mistry   C: ketan mistry
A: dubbed creative   M: hello@dubbedcreative.com

www.vai-fashion.com
D: patrik de jong   C: patrik de jong   P: dirk hoffmann
A: artificialduck studios   M: info@vai-fashion.com

www.rolf-ebitsch.net
D: maren prokopowitsch
M: mail@prokopowitsch.de

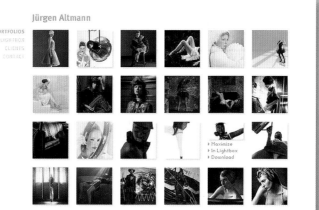

www.juergenaltmann.com
D: benjamin voigtländer   C: florian hauser
A: cosmoto   M: fh@cosmoto.com

www.werecommend.se

D: martin fredricson, nikolaj knop   C: we recommend   P: we recommend
A: we recommend   M: mail@werecommend.se

www.turncodeintobeauty.com

D: stefan grüner   C: stefan grüner
A: turncodeintobeauty.com   M: sg@turncodeintobeauty.com

www.pillowhead.net

D: benjamin robert, candace renee
A: pillowhead   M: hello@pillowhead.net

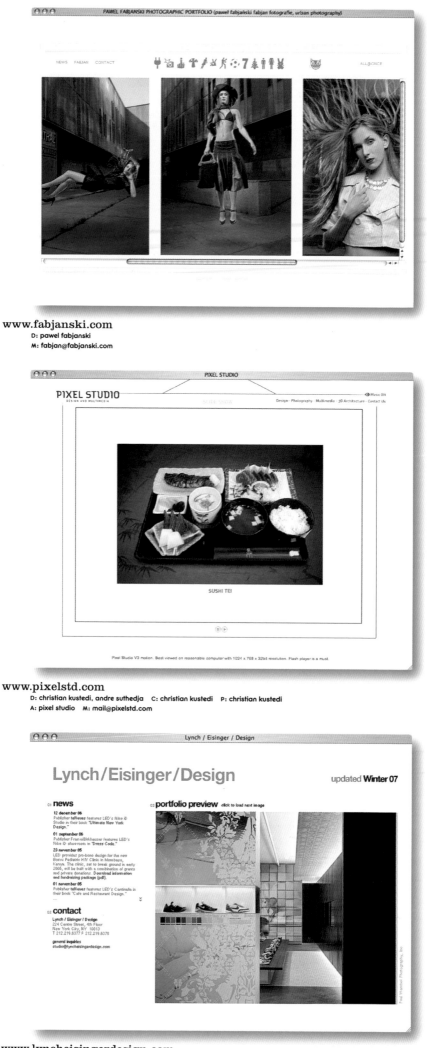

www.fabjanski.com

D: pawel fabjanski
M: fabjan@fabjanski.com

www.pixelstd.com

D: christian kustedi, andre suthedja   C: christian kustedi   P: christian kustedi
A: pixel studio   M: mail@pixelstd.com

www.lyncheisingerdesign.com

D: lynch / eisinger / design   C: christopher connock   P: simon eisinger, christian lynch
A: lynch / eisinger / design   M: studio@lyncheisingerdesign.com

www.pepkarsten.com
D: pep karsten
M: info@pepkarsten.com

www.conservation-architect.co.uk
D: sam dallyn   C: andy biggs
M: samdallyn@hotmail.com

www.cinabro.it
D: gian luca proietti
A: cinabro   M: info@cinabro.it

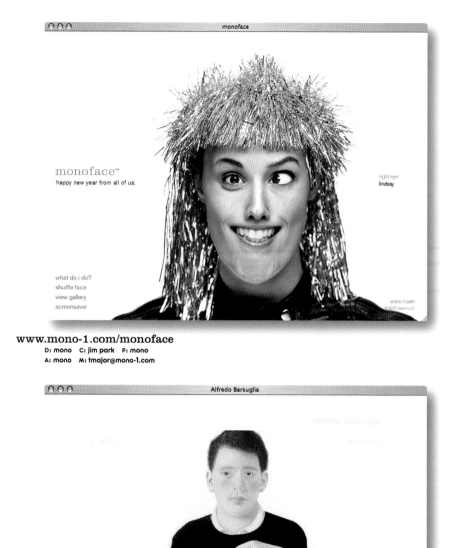

www.mono-1.com/monoface
D: mono   C: jim park   P: mono
A: mono   M: tmajor@mono-1.com

www.alfredobarsuglia.com
D: katja ratschiller   C: markus angerer   P: alexander baldele
A: nyxas   M: office@nyxas.com

www.felicegold.com
D: you, chang-jae   C: hur, jung su   P: you, chang-jae
A: l&f design   M: lnfdesign@naver.com

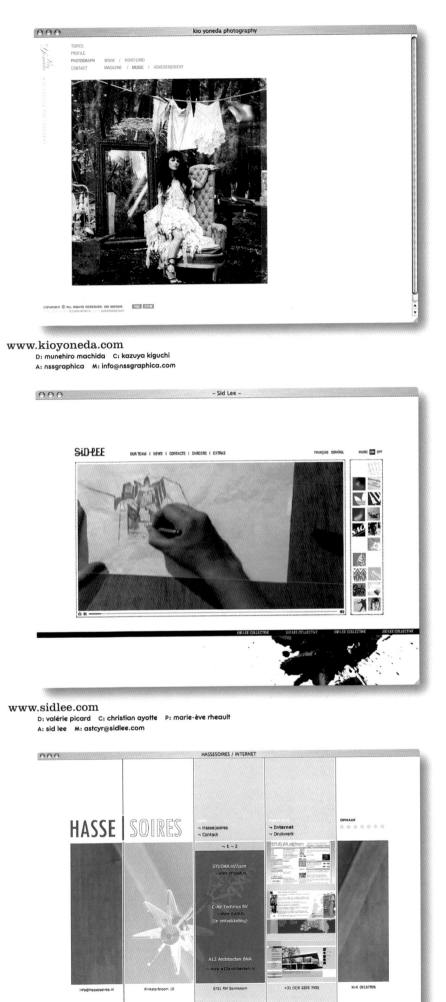

www.kioyoneda.com
D: munehiro machida   C: kazuya kiguchi
A: nssgraphica   M: info@nssgraphica.com

www.sidlee.com
D: valérie picard   C: christian ayotte   P: marie-ève rheault
A: sid lee   M: astcyr@sidlee.com

www.hassesoires.nl
D: arnout hasselaar   C: arnout hasselaar   P: arnout hasselaar
A: hassesoires   M: info@hassesoires.nl

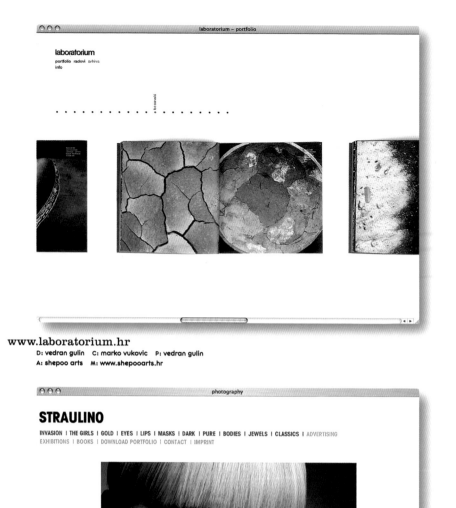

www.laboratorium.hr
D: vedran gulin   C: marko vukovic   P: vedran gulin
A: shepoo arts   M: www.shepooarts.hr

www.straulino.com
D: a. meyer-roxlau   C: sirup°   P: sirup°
A: sirup° agentur für neue medien   M: contact@sirup-media.com

www.metaphrenie.com
D: andrea dionisio, mike helmle   C: simon schories   P: metaphrenie
A: metaphrenie   M: info@metaphrenie.com

www.castit.dk

D: pelle martin   C: kim lynge   P: pelle martin

A: in2media a/s   M: pmc@in2media.dk

www.inlain.ch

D: marianne luck   C: marianne luck   P: marco und dario cadonau

A: südostschweiz newmedia ag, trimarca ag   M: info@newmedia.ch

www.ubaldopantani.it

D: rino s. sassi   C: rino s. sassi   P: rino s. sassi

A: monokraft   M: www.monokraft.com

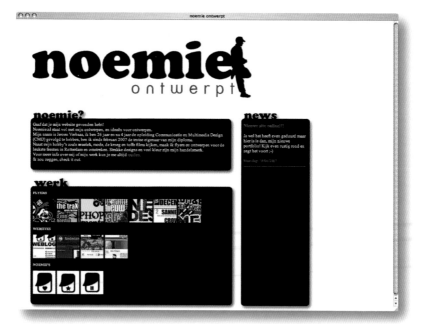

www.noemie.nl

D: jeroen verbaas   C: jeroen verbaas   P: jeroen verbaas
M: info@noemie.nl

www.imin.de

D: jan weiss   C: jan weiss
M: yes@imin.de

www.heikomueller.de

D: heiko müller   C: heiko müller   P: heiko müller
M: info@heikomueller.de

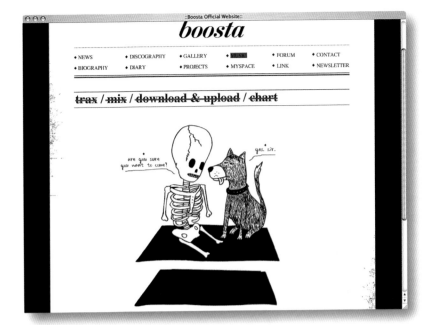

www.boosta.dj
D: blanco   C: blanco   P: blanco
A: blanco   M: info@studioblanco.it

www.syruphelsinki.com
D: antti hinkula, teemu suviala   C: timo koro   P: syrup helsinki
A: syrup helsinki   M: office@syruphelsinki.com

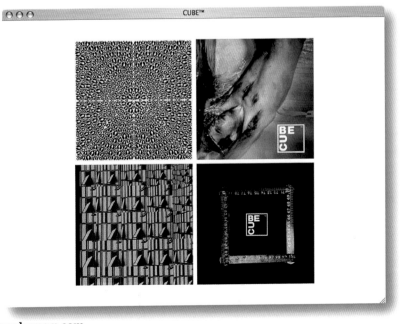

www.cubemag.com
D: giorgio de mitri   C: getto aquino   P: sartoria comunicazione
A: sartoria comunicazione   M: info@sartoria.com

www.mymoleskine.net

D: fabio iaschi   C: fabio iaschi   P: fabio iaschi
A: torakiki   M: info@mymoleskine.net

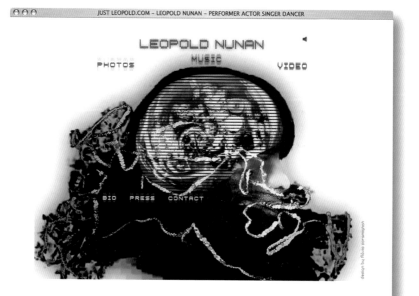

www.justleopold.com

D: flavio scramignon   C: flavio scramignon   P: leopold nunan
M: scramignon@gmail.com

www.wouldyoulikeawebsite.com

D: matt sundstrom, sabina hahn   C: shea gonyo, josh ott   P: mark ferdman
A: freedom interactive design   M: sales@freedominteractivedesign.com

www.unllocunmon.com

D: david resplandí, jordi lafebre   C: cocobongo artworks

A: cocobongo artworks   M: cocobongo@ccbng.com

www.freefarm.co.uk

D: universal everything   C: kleber   P: simon pyke

A: freefarm   M: simon@freefarm.co.uk

www.studiokumorfos.com

D: fred bernier   C: fred bernier   P: fred bernier

A: studio kumorfos   M: contact@kumorfos.com

www.reconq.de
D: jan kromarek   C: jkr   P: jkr
M: jkr@reconq.de

www.taplabs.com
D: mark taplin   C: mark taplin   P: mark taplin
A: taplabs.com   M: tap@taplabs.com

www.welcometo.as
D: adam machacek, sébastien bohner   C: sébastien bohner, joël amaudruz   P: welcometo.as
A: welcometo.as   M: mail@welcometo.as

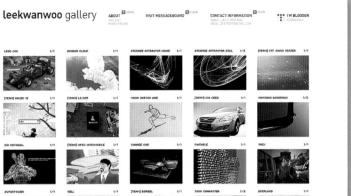

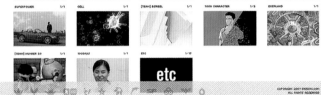

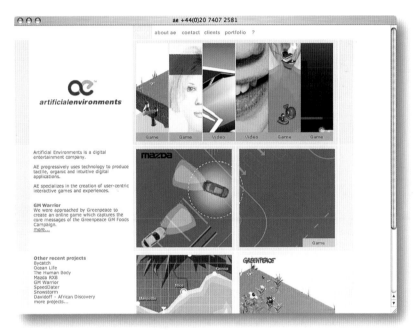

www.dnabox.com

D: leekwanwoo
M: 29.97frame@gmail.com

www.ae-pro.com

D: tom elsner   C: tom elsner, christian knutsson
A: artificial environments   M: tom@ae-pro.com

www.saisondor.com

D: nicolas duprat, vincent périllat, christophe grunenwald
A: saison d'or   M: agence@saisondor.com

71

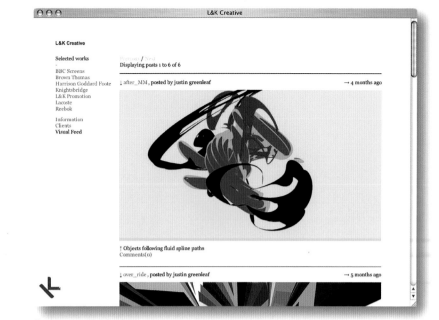

www.landkcreative.com
D: l&k creative
M: mg@landkcreative.com

www.spencerwilson.co.uk
D: spencer wilson   C: www.sennep.com   P: www.sennep.com
M: spencer@spencerwilson.co.uk

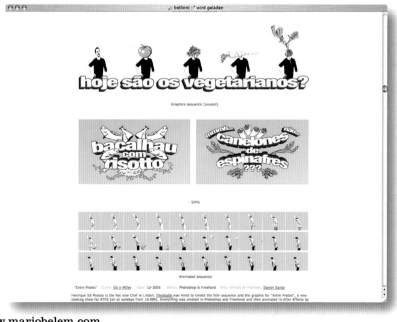

www.mariobelem.com
D: mario belem   C: mario belem   P: mario belem
A: mario belem   M: m@mariobelem.com

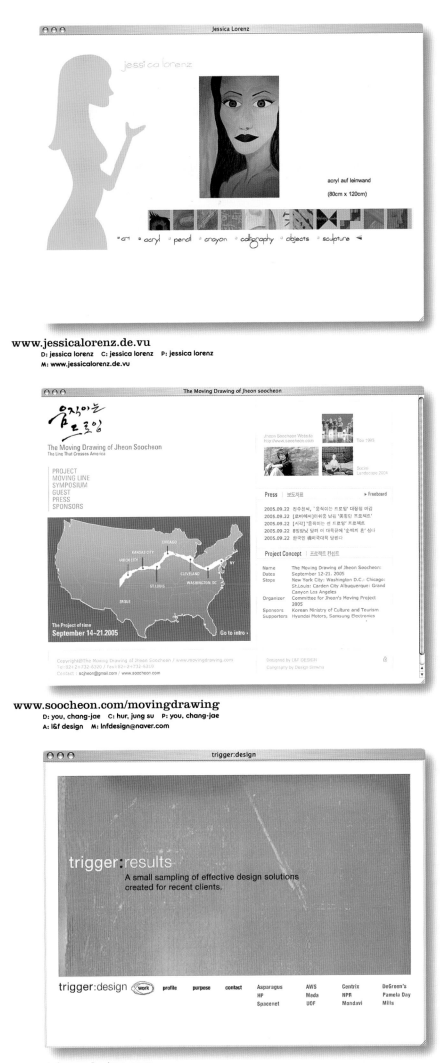

www.jessicalorenz.de.vu
D: jessica lorenz   C: jessica lorenz   P: jessica lorenz
M: www.jessicalorenz.de.vu

www.soocheon.com/movingdrawing
D: you, chang-jae   C: hur, jung su   P: you, chang-jae
A: l&f design   M: lnfdesign@naver.com

www.triggerdesign.com
D: matthew rowland, matt sanders   C: matt sanders   P: matt sanders
A: trigger design   M: info@triggerdesign.com

www.nomoreclones.co.uk
D: ross turner   C: ross turner   P: ross turner
A: no more clones   M: ross@nomoreclones.co.uk

www.natruc.com
D: jiří pálka   C: jiří pálka   P: jiří pálka
M: palka.jiri@centrum.cz

www.cerveceros.org
D: estefanía pérez huerga
M: www.ra-marketing.com

www.charlenechua.com

D: charlene chua   C: charlene chua, lokesh dhakar   P: charlene chua

A: charlene chua, illustration   M: charlene@charlenechua.com

www.momosi.com

D: min kyung seo   C: min kyung seo   P: min kyung seo

A: momosi   M: min@momosi.com

www.creationdance.co.uk

D: stefania boiano   C: netdood   P: creation dance studio

A: netdood   M: info@netdood.com

www.isabelpinto.com

D: dominik seeger   C: ernest and edgar   P: isabel pinto
A: isabel pinto fotografia   M: isabel@isabelpinto.com

www.gluesociety.com

D: the glue society
M: hello@gluesociety.com

www.smallfriescookbook.com

D: teri cambell, josh barnes, brandon blangger, brian keenan
A: openfield creative   M: opendialogue@openfieldcreative.com

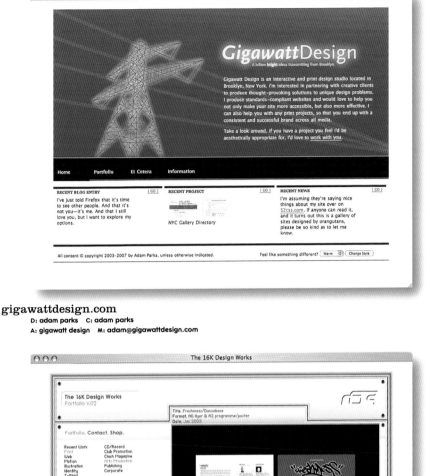

gigawattdesign.com
D: adam parks   C: adam parks
A: gigawatt design   M: adam@gigawattdesign.com

www.16kdesign.com
D: paul galbraith   C: paul galbraith   P: john anderson
A: the 16k design works   M: info@16kdesign.com

www.tennisclubgenova.it
D: ilaria boz   C: maurizio albertoni
A: dps s.r.l.   M: info@dpsonline.it

COMPO 024
BARCELONA, 2005
36" x 24"

◻ ART PORTFOLIO | PORTFOLIO D'ART
◻ DESIGN PORTFOLIO | PORTFOLIO DE DESIGN
◻ BIOGRAPHY | BIOGRAPHIE
◻ MY BLOG | MON BLOG
◻ CONTACT | CONTACT
◻ HOME | ACCUEIL

All arts are for sale. Various sizes are available.
For a complete portfolio or to commision a special request, send her an _email_.
Les oeuvres sont à vendre. Plusieurs formats sont disponibles.
Pour un portfolio complet ou des commandes spéciales, envoyez-lui un _courriel_.

www.nouknouk.com
D: roxana brongo   C: julie baribeau
M: roxana@nouknouk.com

the Natural Remedy
for small and big
health troubles

D | Skip menu | Italiano

⚘ Home
⚘ History and origins
⚘ Composition
⚘ Applications
⚘ FAQ
⚘ Doctor Gotti
⚘ Doctor Chamachai
⚘ Site contents

🌼 Trat Yellow Oil

Are you looking for a single, natural product relieving everyday big and little pains, without hurting your organism?

You have found it - it is the Yellow Oil, a wellness oil. It is an original formula from the oriental traditional medicine, handed down through the generations as a cure-all and currently appreciated by doctors as well.

Applications
Some examples of the main applications of hte Yellow Oil as a substitute of the common and more harmful medicines, in the treatment of many health troubles.

View Applications »

History and origins
The origins and the history of the Yellow Oil, with a short introduction to the main differences between Western Medicine and Chinese Traditional Medicine.

View History and Origins »

FAQ
Some frequently asked questions useful to understand the characteristics and the possible uses of the "Yellow Oil" wellness oil.

View FAQ »

Sale points
Yellow Oil is available for sale in all Italian pharmacy and herb shop.

Angelo Gotti - Medico Chirurgo P.IVA 00163390596 | Privacy Policy | Confinigrafici design

www.oliogiallo.it
D: orietta verdiani   C: giuseppe tongiani   P: dott. angelo gotti
A: confinigrafici   M: www.confinigrafici.it

PUB CHIMENEA (Porriño)
Creación de una nueva imagen para un estandarte de las noches de ocio de Porriño. Proyecto en el cual debíamos reformar el local teniendo en cuenta los gustos de una clientela fiel que venía identificándose con la imagen que debíamos transformar.

LA EMPRESA
SERVICIOS
TRABAJOS
MODESTO HERMIDA

La Guía, 24. Oficina 5 • Atios • 36418 PORRIÑO (Pontevedra) • Telf: 986 348 407   Nota legal - © Dreitec 2007

www.modestohermida.es
D: adolo maragoto   C: miguel abal   P: juan luis hermo
A: dretec sl   M: info@dreitec.com

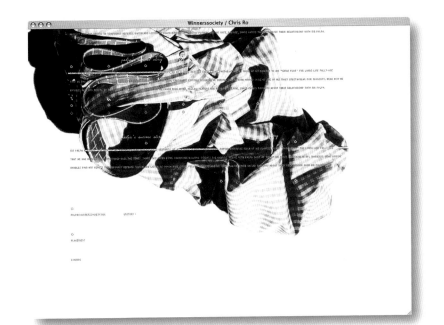

www.winnerssociety.org
D: chris ro
A: adearfriend™ M: ro@winnerssociety.org

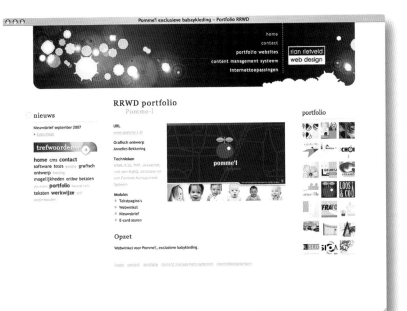

www.rrwd.nl
D: debby van dongen C: rian rietveld P: debby van dongen, rian rietveld
A: conk M: info@conk.nl

www.cbs.polyu.edu.hk
D: teresa l.y. lee C: ivan yeung, yat-yu wu
A: compelite M: info@compelite.net

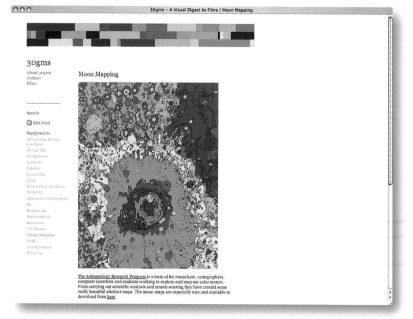

www.30gms.com

D: david rainbird, vikesh bhatt   C: steve sharpe   P: liz greening
A: fibre   M: hello@30gms.com

www.oasim.com

D: oasim karmieh   C: oasim karmieh   P: oasim karmieh
A: oasim karmieh   M: pixelbudah@gmail.com

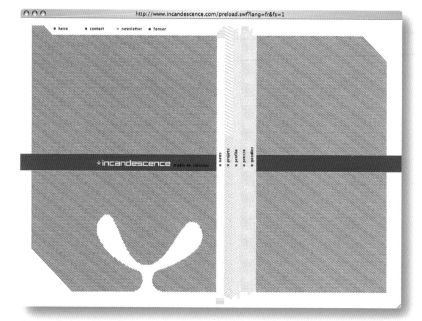

www.incandescence.com

D: etienne mineur   C: etienne mineur
A: incandescence   M: etienne@incandescence.com

www.walkcycle.com
D: cybèle   C: cybèle   P: cybèle
A: cybèle illustration   M: cybele@walkcycle.com

www.dvdrent.sk
D: pavel surovi   C: pavel surovi   P: pavel surovi
A: communication agency   M: info@communicationagency.com

www.ff0066.com
D: raphy fedida   C: raphy fedida
M: raphy@ff0066.com

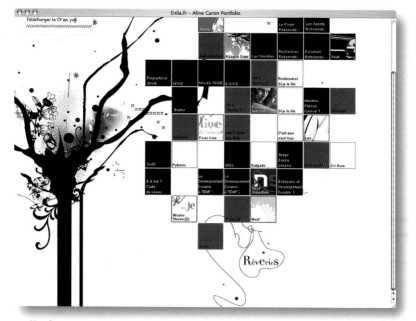

www.enila.fr
D: aline caron   C: antoine ughetto
M: aline.caron@gmail.com

www.plasticsoda.com
D: vegard bjørlykke
M: vegard@plasticsoda.com

www.bizzdesign.de
D: daniela boudgoust   C: daniela boudgoust
A: bizz design company   M: boudgoust@bizzdesign.de

www.athmosfera.it
D: giacomo giancarlo C: andrea frattaruolo P: giacomo giancarlo
A: kynetos s.r.l. M: www.kynetos.com

www.gonsa.cl
D: nexprochile P: gonsa
A: nexprochile M: info@nexprochile.cl

www.fkinteractive.com
D: hans spooren P: max oshman
A: fk interactive, llc M: info@fkinteractive.com

www.planetapluton.com

D: david sueiro
A: buenas ideas en accion sl   M: info@planetapluton.com

www.sellroom.de

D: markus spiske   C: achim schmidt   P: markus spiske, achim schmidt
A: temporausch - kommunikation & photography   M: info@temporausch.com

www.uco.es/agenda

D: rafael crespín   C: rafael crespín   P: corduba university
A: corduba university   M: q72crcrr@uco.es

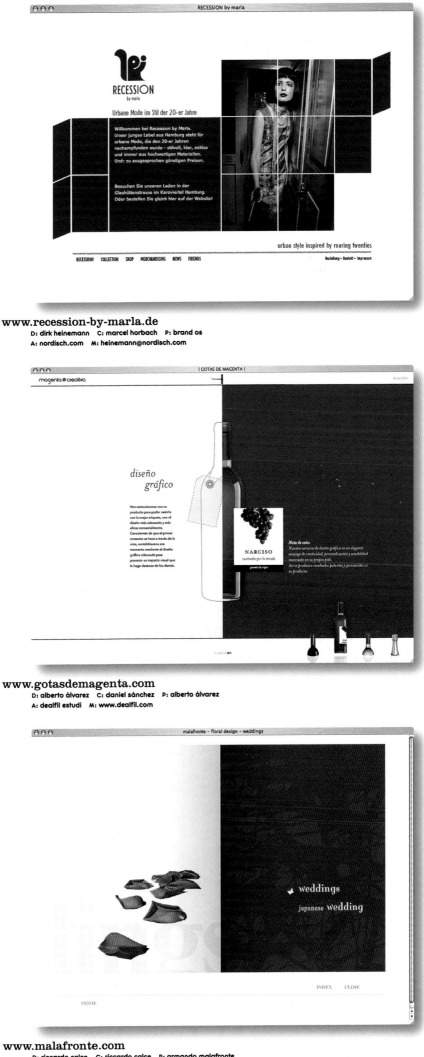

www.recession-by-marla.de
D: dirk heinemann   C: marcel horbach   P: brand os
A: nordisch.com   M: heinemann@nordisch.com

www.gotasdemagenta.com
D: alberto álvarez   C: daniel sánchez   P: alberto álvarez
A: dealfil estudi   M: www.dealfil.com

www.malafronte.com
D: riccardo calce   C: riccardo calce   P: armando malafronte
A: quidp   M: riccardo.calce@quidp.com

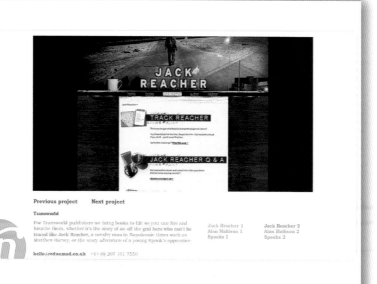

www.rednomad.co.uk
D: xyn xu   C: jon parkinson   P: gina russell
A: red nomad   M: hello@rednomad.co.uk

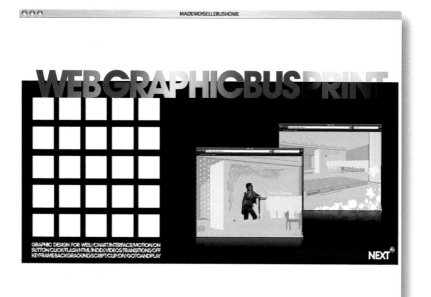

www.mademoisellebus.fr
D: rose de ménibus   C: rose de ménibus   P: rose de ménibus
M: contact@mademoisellebus.fr

www.sergeseidlitz.com
D: serge seidlitz   C: serge seidlitz   P: serge seidlitz
A: serge seidlitz   M: mail@sergeseidlitz.com

www.eyevisuals.com
D: robin van de putte
A: eyevisuals all media   M: info@eyevisuals.com

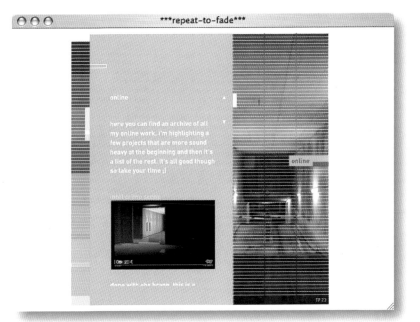

www.repeat-to-fade.net
D: thomas poeser, owen lloyd   C: thomas poeser   P: owen lloyd
A: tp23   M: owen@repeat-to-fade.net

www.ditapepe.cz
D: milan nedv   C: jiri petvaldsky
A: men at work   M: milan@m-a-w.cz

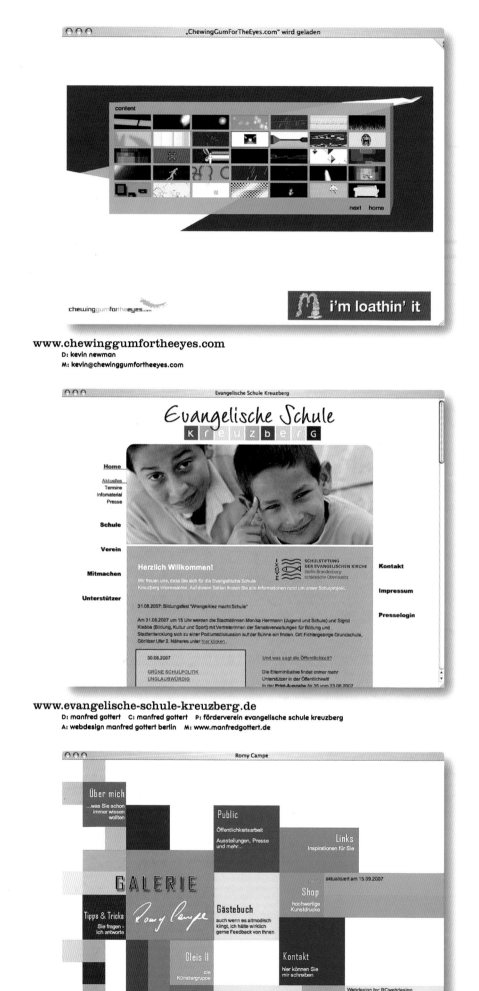

www.chewinggumfortheeyes.com
D: kevin newman
M: kevin@chewinggumfortheeyes.com

www.evangelische-schule-kreuzberg.de
D: manfred gottert   C: manfred gottert   P: förderverein evangelische schule kreuzberg
A: webdesign manfred gottert berlin   M: www.manfredgottert.de

www.romycampe.de
D: romy campe   C: romy campe   P: romy campe
A: rcwebdesign   M: info@rcwebdesign.de

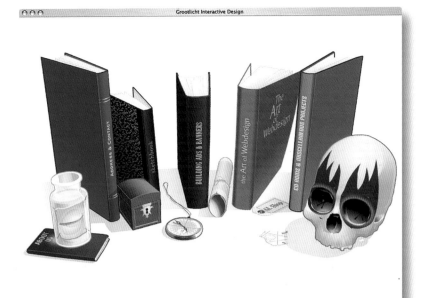

www.grootlicht.com

D: ivo van de grift   C: ivo van de grift, ivo domburg   P: ivo van de grift
A: grootlicht interactive design   M: info@grootlicht.com

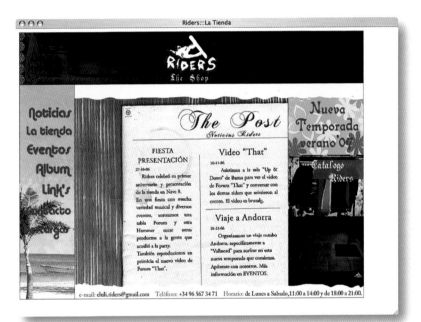

www.riders.es

D: luis manuel mas orts, alejandro hostalet   C: miguel cartagena, carlos maciá
M: ecologik@gmail.com

www.hkaff.com.hk

D: john chan, pam hung
A: postgal.com   M: postgal@gmail.com

www.agenciatrendy.com
D: jeff león   C: jeff león   P: jeff león
A: trendypose ltda.   M: jeff@agenciatrendy.com

www.born05.nl
D: sjors van hoof, mickel van kouwen   C: mickel van kouwen   P: rogier ijzermans
A: born05   M: rogier@born05.nl

www.mfdsa.cl
D: nexprochile   P: macro food
A: nexprochile   M: info@nexprochile.cl

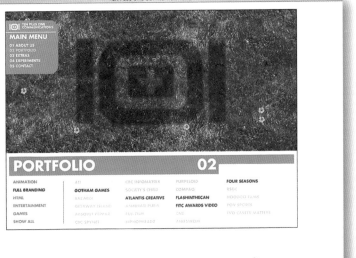

www.10plus1.com

D: ryan wolman   C: mike nowak, john park, angela lee   P: david bastedo
A: ten plus one communications inc.   M: david@10plus1.com

www.mschwarzer.com

D: m. schwarzer   C: tobias menzel   P: m. schwarzer
M: cuntact@mschwarzer.com

www.zaumlab.com

D: guido baratta   C: giovanni manca   P: zaumlab
A: zaum | handmade portable fashion   M: gbar@zaumlab.com

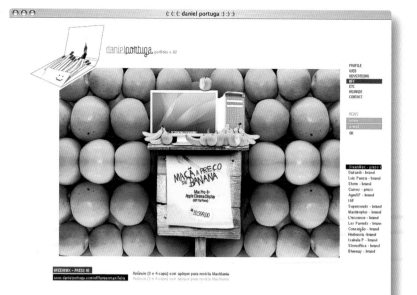

www.danielportuga.com

D: daniel "portuga", l. sousa   C: ítalo borges
M: portuga@danielportuga.com

www.bravomuebles.com

D: bravo!, barbara elías   C: sebastián aguila   P: sebastián aguila
A: monolab   M: www.monolab.cl

www.mayastepien.nl

D: maya stepien   C: joost wouterse
M: maya@mayastepien.nl

www.blueart.it

D: leonardo simiani   C: gianni sicchitiello   P: leonardo simiani
A: blue art s.r.l.   M: info@blueart.it

www.eyedentitygames.com

D: nikita lee
M: info@eyedentitygames.com

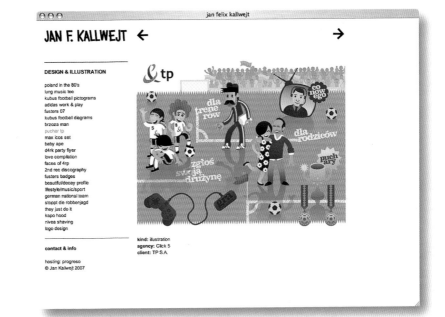

www.kallwejt.com

D: jan kallwejt   C: jens hinrichs   P: jan kallwejt
M: jan@kallwejt.com

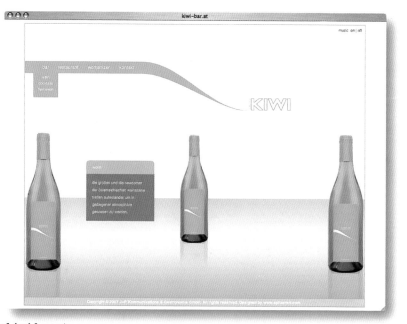

www.universalcomunicacion.com
D: david   P: mario
A: universal comunicacion   M: www.universalcomunicacion.com

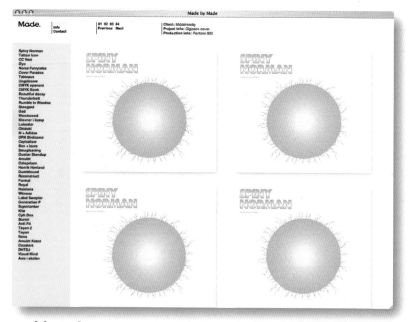

www.kiwi-bar.at
D: matthias spitzer   C: www.druckdichaus.de   P: matthias spitzer
A: agentur_07   M: office@agentur07.com

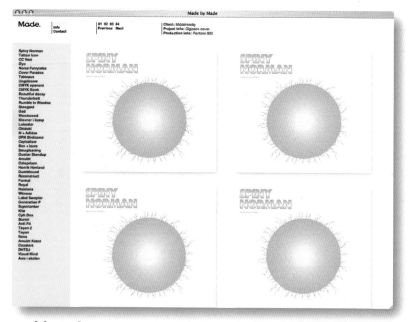

www.madebymade.no
D: made   C: marius wold   P: made
A: made   M: info@madebymade.no

www.clockwork.no

D: espen linna

A: edison interactive - www.edison.no   M: espen@edison.no

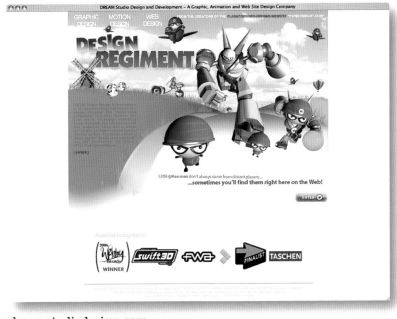

www.dreamstudiodesign.com

D: danny hetzroni   C: danny hetzroni   P: danny hetzroni

A: dream studio design   M: info@dreamstudiodesign.com

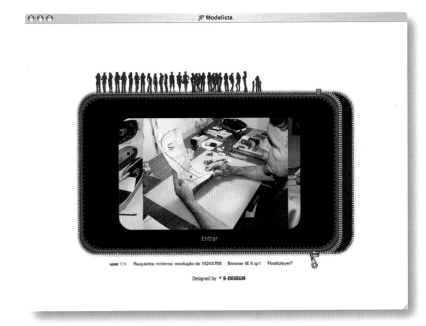

www.joper.pt.vu

D: sara m da costa pinho   C: daniela cláudia m correia   P: sara pinho, daniela correia

A: s-design   M: sdesignproj@hotmail.com

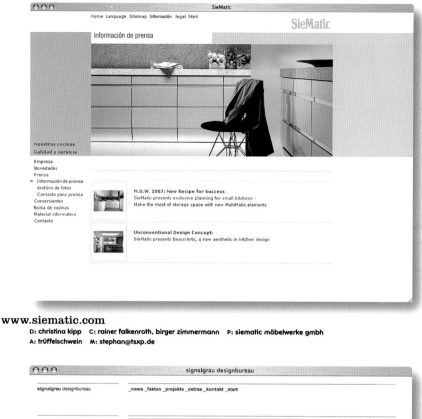

www.siematic.com
D: christina kipp   C: rainer falkenroth, birger zimmermann   P: siematic möbelwerke gmbh
A: trüffelschwein   M: stephan@tsxp.de

www.signalgrau.com
D: dirk uhlenbrock   C: dirk uhlenbrock   P: dirk uhlenbrock
A: signalgrau designbureau   M: uhlenbrock@signalgrau.com

www.marekhaiduk.de
D: marek haiduk
M: telegramm@marekhaiduk.de

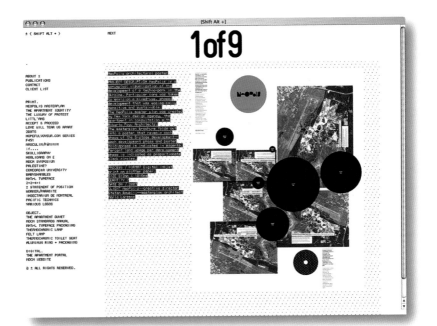

plusminus.ca

D: peter crnokrak C: peter crnokrak P: peter crnokrak

A: ± M: info@plusminus.ca

www.suli.at

D: michaela kerschbaum C: daniela strassberger P: snowboardschule suli

A: datenkraft M: www.datenkraft.com

www.etkon.de

D: severin brettmeister

A: fa-ro marketing gmbh M: www.etkon.de

www.tta.it/tta.htm

D: libero cavinato   C: libero cavinato   P: libero cavinato

A: liberonline   M: libero@liberonline.com

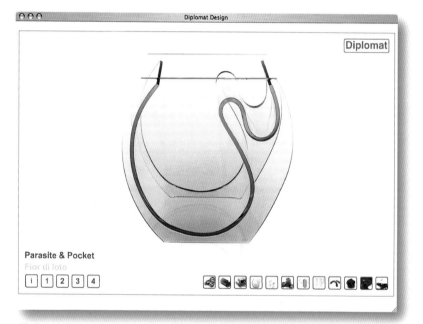

www.diplomatdesign.com

D: diplomat   C: aaron bennett   P: aaron bennett

A: aaron bennett designs   M: info@diplomatdesign.com

www.pousadacaju.com

D: luis kapinha   C: hugo vicente   P: luis kapinha

A: terradesign   M: info@pousadacaju.com

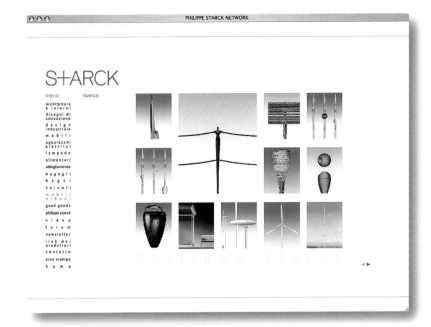

www.starcknetwork.com
D: philippe starck   C: markus kern
A: web workstyle   M: info@web-workstyle.com

www.eugene-and-louise.be
D: glenn d'hondt, sylvia meert   C: studio plum   P: glenn d'hondt, sylvia meert
A: eugene and louise   M: info@eugene-and-louise.be

www.bridgemedia.co.uk
D: matt etherington   C: matt etherington   P: matt etherington
A: bridge media   M: www.bridgemedia.co.uk

www.simonrasmussen.com
D: kristian grove møller   C: felix nielsen
A: kriss créol   M: kgm@krisscreol.com

www.coreyfishes.com
D: corey arnold   C: mieko saito   P: corey arnold
A: coreyfishes inc.   M: corey@coreyfishes.com

www.gioiacosmetics.com
D: vicky perales, marcos cevasco   C: vicky perales   P: vicky perales
A: vicperales design   M: vicperales@vicperales.com.ar

puzzleroad.apoka.com

D: edouard artus   C: edouard artus   P: edouard artus
A: apoka   M: artus@apoka.com

www.pistoletbleu.com

D: chino, claude bernard   C: chino is julien cave   P: claude bernard
A: studio pistolet bleu, cafe creme   M: contact@pistoletbleu.com

www.oddwall.com

D: stephen ensminger   C: stephen ensminger
M: saintx@oddwall.com

www.bauer-gamlitz.at

D: daniela strassberger C: daniela strassberger P: karl bauer
A: daniela strassberger M: www.daniela-strassberger.net

www.lotie.com

D: julien blanchet C: julien blanchet, stéphane colliège P: rezo zero
A: rezo zero M: contact@lotie.com

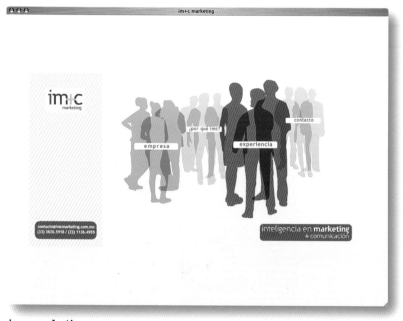

www.imcmarketing.com.mx

D: calderon preciado, juan pablo C: calderon preciado, juan pablo P: raya, carlos
A: imc marketing M: pablogeminis@hotmail.com

www.simsnow.com

D: ian coyle   C: ian coyle   P: matt fajohn
A: fl2, superheroes   M: ian@superhero.es

www.vicperales.com.ar

D: vicky perales   C: vicky perales   P: vicky perales, dario vulpes
A: vicperales creative factory   M: vicperales@vicperales.com.ar

www.tiowebsolutions.com

D: steven guzman
A: intergraphicdesigns, tiowebsolutions   M: www.tiowebsolutions.com

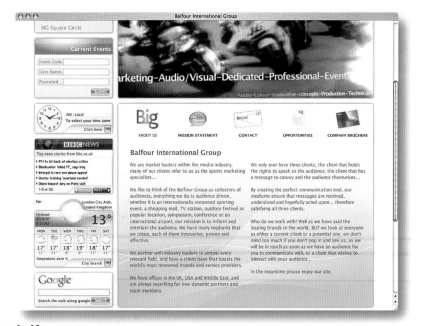

www.balfourgroup.com
D: danny burnside   C: chris sees, george medve   P: stella jordan
A: square circle media   M: www.sqcircle.com

www.uc.be
D: fabian aerts, jurgen houben, werner neirinckx
M: werner.neirinckx@uc.be

www.pocoyo.com
D: daniel sanllehi, oscar garcía   C: d.sanllehi, l.armengol   P: colman lópez, d.cantolla
A: zinkia entertainment   M: host@zinkia.com

nitzsche.info

D: stefan nitzsche   C: stefan nitzsche   P: stefan nitzsche
A: stefan nitzsche   M: stefan@nitzsche.info

www.paulolsman.nl

D: paul olsman   C: paul olsman
M: paul@paulolsman.nl

www.inah.gob.mx/ninos/inah_chicos/index.html

D: margarito lázaro mendoza   P: instituto nacional de antropología e historia
M: b_liquido@hotmail.com

www.cmdcreativo.com
D: cecilia cortés contreras   C: cecilia cortés contreras   P: cecilia cortés contreras
A: creatividad, marketing y diseño s.c.   M: info@cmdcreativo.com

www.lowbudget.pl
D: filip kozarski, piotr ruszkowski, maciej ryniewicz   C: tomasz tjfk kuczma
A: lowbudget   M: info@lowbudget.pl

www.aquaringweb.eu
D: jonathan brennan
M: brennanjonathan@yahoo.co.uk

www.coufal.ch

D: daniela strassberger   C: daniela strassberger   P: hanspeter coufal
A: daniela strassberger   M: www.daniela-strassberger.net

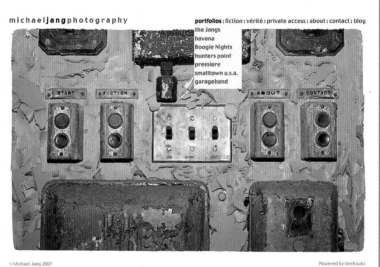

www.michaeljang.com

D: michael jang   C: michael jang   P: michael jang
A: michael jang   M: look@michaeljang.com

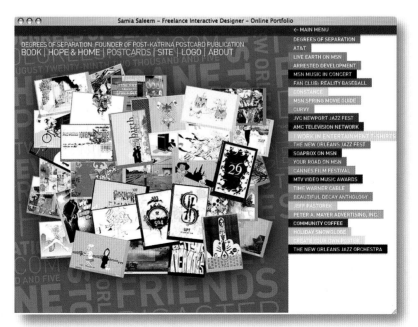

www.samiasaleem.com

D: samia saleem
A: samia saleem   M: samia@aplural.com

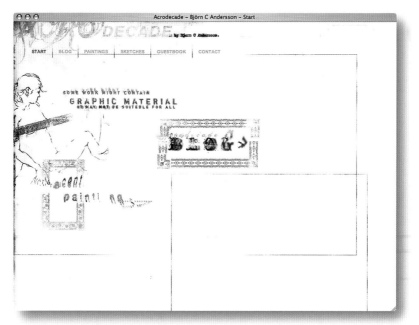

www.acrodecade.com

D: björn c andersson   C: andreas brandell   P: björn c andersson
M: bjorn.andersson@acrodecade.com

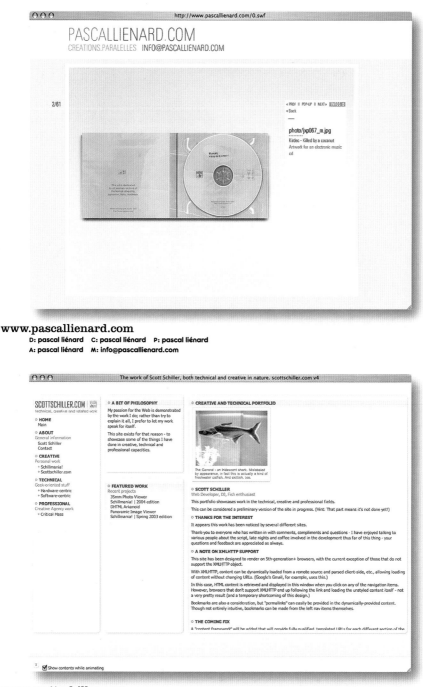

www.pascallienard.com

D: pascal liénard   C: pascal liénard   P: pascal liénard
A: pascal liénard   M: info@pascallienard.com

www.scottschiller.com

D: scott schiller   C: scott schiller
M: s@schillmania.com

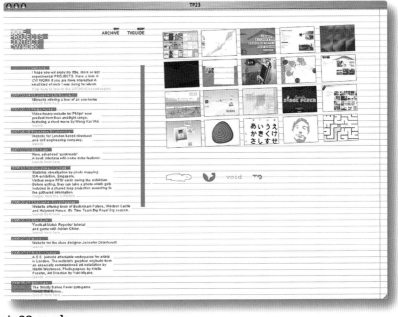

www.tp23.co.uk
D: thomas poeser   C: thomas poeser   P: thomas poeser
A: tp23   M: info@tp23.co.uk

www.vdetegels.be
D: luc mauws   P: dirk tavernier
A: mauws & tavernier bvba   M: dirk@mt-interactive.com

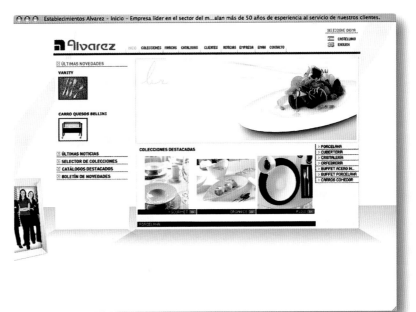

www.alvarez.es
D: toni sánchez   C: philipp keweloh   P: juan carlos rodriguez
A: probalear   M: diseno@probalear.info

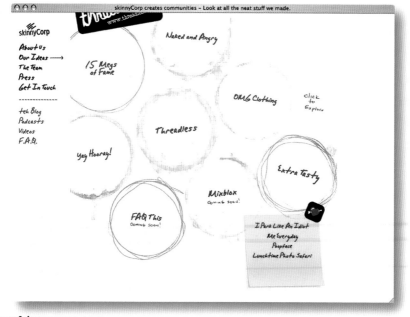

www.skinnycorp.com
D: jeffrey kalmikoff C: jake nickell
A: skinnycorp M: jeffrey@skinnycorp.com

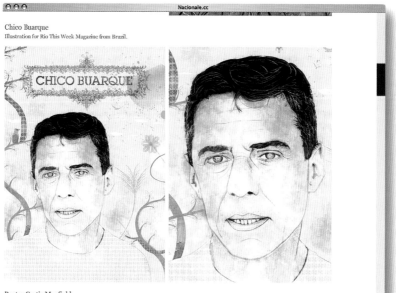

Chico Buarque
Illustration for Rio This Week Magazine from Brazil.

Poster Curtis Mayfield

www.nacionale.cc
D: doug alves C: keita kun
A: nacionale™ M: hello@nacionale.cc

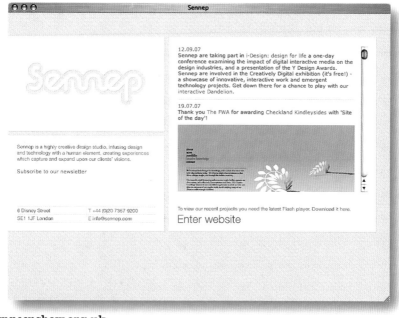

www.peepshow.org.uk
D: matt rice C: sennep P: sennep, peepshow
A: peepshow M: info@peepshow.org.uk

www.fiftyeight.com

D: stephan lauhoff, sascha koeth   C: martin kraft, alex wenz   P: fiftyeight 3d
A: 3deluxe motion   M: marc@fiftyeight.com

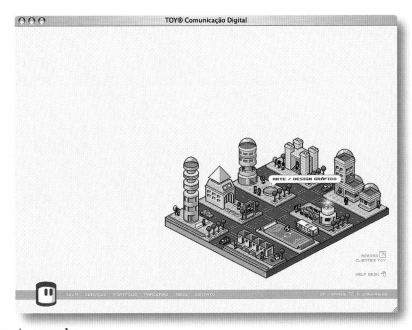

www.gekus.com

D: georg rienzner   C: georg rienzner   P: georg rienzner
A: gekus   M: info@gekus.com

www.toy.com.br

D: renato di giorgio   C: renato di giorgio   P: renato di giorgio
A: toy comunicação digital   M: renato@toy.com.br

111

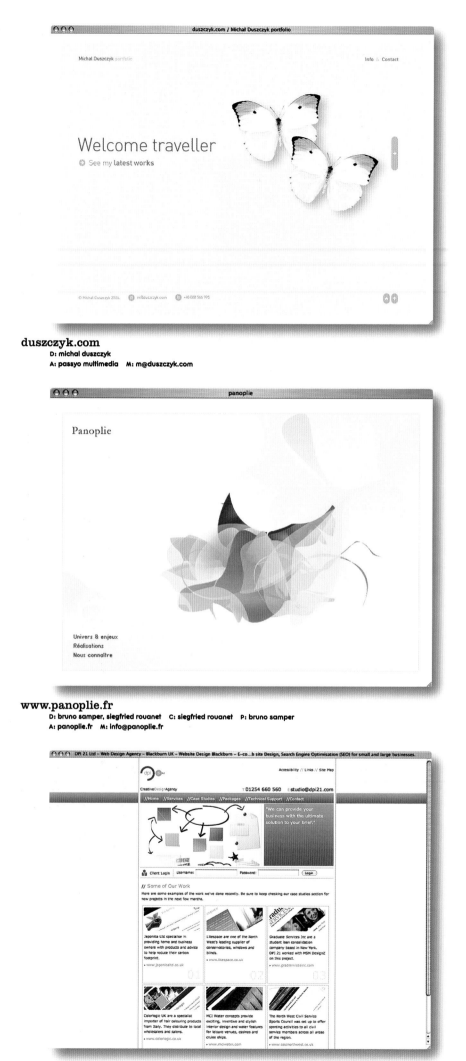

duszczyk.com
D: michal duszczyk
A: passyo multimedia   M: m@duszczyk.com

www.panoplie.fr
D: bruno samper, siegfried rouanet   C: siegfried rouanet   P: bruno samper
A: panoplie.fr   M: info@panoplie.fr

www.dpi21.com
D: steven taylor   C: dpi 21   P: dpi 21
A: dpi 21 ltd   M: studio@dpi21.com

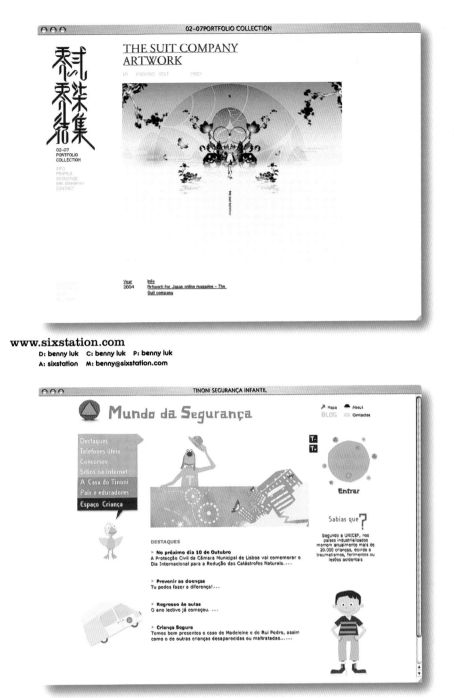

THE SUIT COMPANY
ARTWORK

1/1   PREVIOUS   NEXT   INDEX

Year	Info
2004	Artwork for Japan online magazine – The Suit company

www.sixstation.com

D: benny luk   C: benny luk   P: benny luk
A: sixstation   M: benny@sixstation.com

TINONI SEGURANÇA INFANTIL

Mundo da Segurança

Mapa   About
BLOG   Contactos

Destaques
Telefones úteis
Concursos
Sítios na internet
A Casa do Tinoni
Pais e educadores
Espaço Criança

T-
T+

Entrar

Sabias que?

Segundo a UNICEF, nos países industrializados morrem anualmente mais de 20.000 crianças, devido a traumatismos, ferimentos ou lesões acidentais

DESTAQUES

➤ **No próximo dia 10 de Outubro**
A Protecção Civil da Câmara Municipal de Lisboa vai comemorar o Dia Internacional para a Redução das Catástrofes Naturais. . . .

➤ **Prevenir as doenças**
Tu podes fazer a diferença! . . .

➤ **Regresso às aulas**
O ano lectivo já começou. . . .

➤ **Criança Segura**
Temos bem presentes o caso de Madeleine e do Rui Pedro, assim como o de outras crianças desaparecidas ou maltratadas... . . .

www.tinoni.com

D: pascal scrivani   P: dedoface
A: câmara municipal de lisboa /departamento protecção civil   M: tinoni@cm-lisboa.pt

Alex Trochut – Creativity, Type & Illustration.

www.alextrochut.com

D: alex trochut   C: roger pau
A: alex trochut sl   M: alex@alextrochut.com

www.criteriondg.info/wordpress
D: armando sotoca   C: alberto carazo
M: armando@criteriondg.info

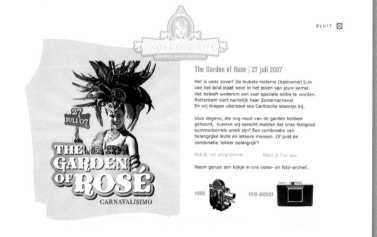

www.morethanlive.nl
D: jaroslav gort   C: sam terburg   P: henk aron
A: more than live - brand experience   M: jaroslav@morethanlive.nl

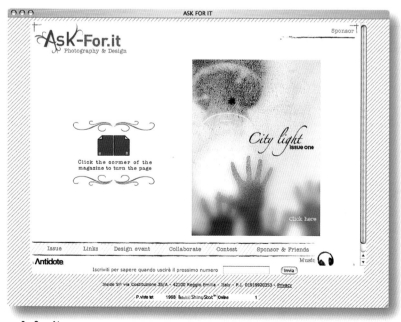

www.ask-for.it
D: guerrieri stefano   C: guerrieri stefano   P: guerrieri stefano
M: www.antidote.it

www.dev-gestalter.de
D: dimitri wittmann, ruben müller
A: devolution gbr   M: info@dev-gestalter.de

www.kokenhof.de
D: saskia pierschek   C: saskia pierschek, tim-oliver schulz
A: iconnewmedia   M: saskia.pierschek@iconnewmedia.de

www.encantado.net
D: brecht acke   C: lloyd moore
A: encantado.net   M: info@encantado.net

www.monasterodibose.it

D: matteo beretta, marco rigon   P: rodolfo rigon, monaci di bose
A: trend up   M: trend@trendup.it

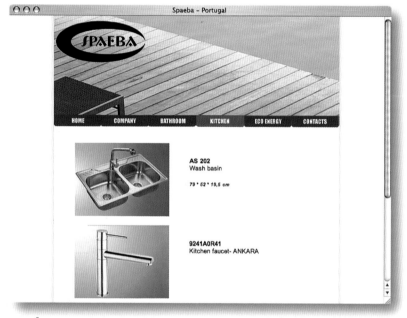

www.spaeba.com

D: flávio gomes   C: flávio gomes   P: flávio gomes
A: flávio gart   M: flavio.gart@gmail.com

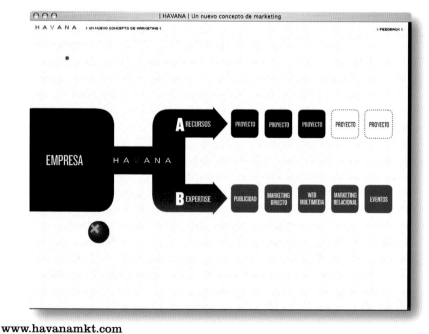

www.havanamkt.com

D: alberto álvarez   C: daniel sánchez   P: alberto álvarez
A: dealfil estudi   M: www.dealfil.com

Dark Meat City (Vol.1 - French only)

Angelino is a young loser just like thousands of others in Dark Meat City. He squats a seedy hotel room in the Latino neighborhood of Rios Rosas. His dreary existence consists of zapping, Mexican wrestling matches (of which he is a devotee), shitty little jobs and so-called metaphysical discussions under the stars with his buddy Vinz. A silly scooter accident is going to plunge Angelino in a whirlwind of improbable troubles putting at stake all of humanity! The manhunt has started, involving massively armed men in black, all sorts of gangs, Mexican wrestlers and even Machos, these vicious cosmic entities determined to invade our planet!!!

Mutafukaz has been inspired by the 50's Sci-Fi mixed with contemporary ingredients such as Hip Hop and wrestling. This cocktail makes it a dark, paranoid but fun comic book.

Mutafukaz counts 124 explosive pages smelling of tacos, cold sweat, bitumen and paranoia as well as an incredible cocktail of Hip Hop, Mexican wrestling and 50's Sci-Fi.

Dark Meat City (Vol.1 - French only)
Story, drawing and colors by RUN
124 color pages.
Release date: 24/08/2006
Selling price: €14.90

» Read the 10 first pages

Buy the first volume online
(in French only)

www.mutafukaz.com
D: run aka guillaume renard   C: run, ankama editions   P: run
A: ankama editions   M: alix@ankama.com

www.steunpuntgok.be
D: leen de smedt, ballyhoo webdesign   C: steunpunt gok   P: steunpunt gok
A: ballyhoo webdesign   M: info@ballyhoo.be

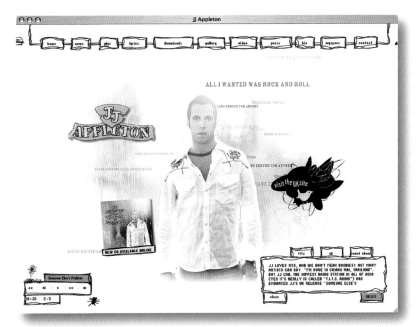

www.jjappleton.com
D: alon zouaretz   C: alon zouaretz   P: lora appleton
A: edge lab   M: lora@edgelabinc.com

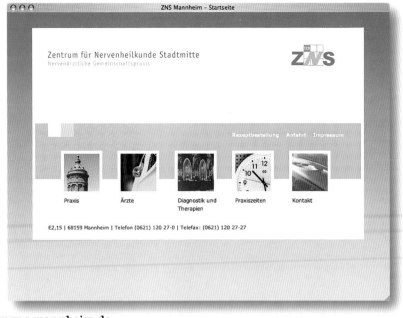

www.zns-mannheim.de
D: sebastian thönnes   C: frank robnik   P: patrick thilmann
A: buscape   M: www.buscape.de

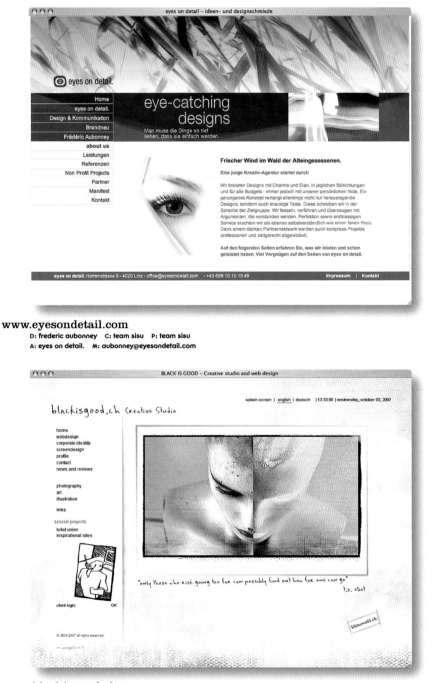

www.eyesondetail.com
D: frederic aubonney   C: team sisu   P: team sisu
A: eyes on detail.   M: aubonney@eyesondetail.com

www.blackisgood.ch
D: doron yefet, edith rosenberg   C: doron yefet
A: black is good - creative studio   M: contact@blackisgood.ch

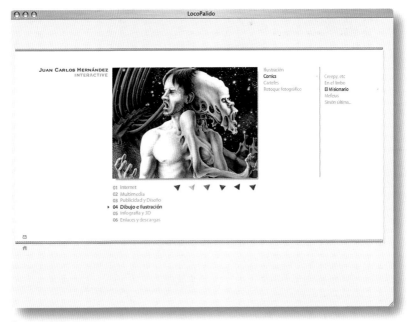

www.locopalido.com
D: juan carlos hernández
M: juancarlos@locopalido.com

www.hcreativos.com
D: juan carlos hernandez camara, einar reyes valdez   C: alfredo bolio
A: hache creativos s.c.p.   M: contacto@hcreativos.com

www.ozhongkong.com
D: teresa l.y. lee   C: eric chan, yat-yu wu
A: compelite   M: info@compelite.net

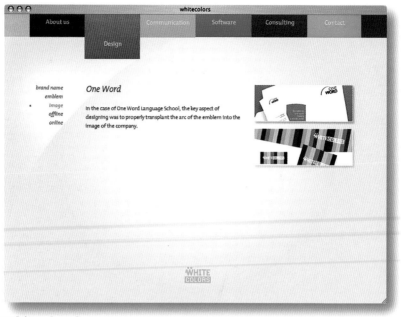

www.whitecolors.hu

D: zoltán csordás C: gergely nyikos P: andrea tóth
A: cenacolo co. - whitecolors M: andras.p@whitecolors.hu

www.energiaedomotica.it

D: francesca morbidelli
A: macom srl M: fmorbi@gmail.com

www.webcenter.am

D: karen meliksetyan C: tigran niksalyan P: karen meliksetyan
A: webcenter M: info@webcenter.am

www.hellomynameis.it
D: alessandro d'alessandro   C: alessandro d'alessandro   P: alessandro d'alessandro
M: dale@hellomynameis.it

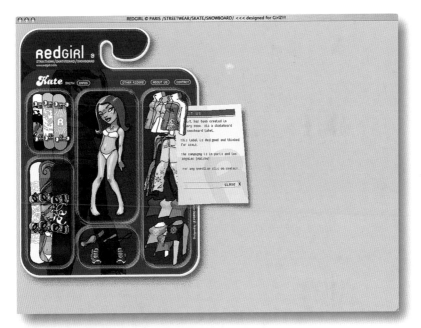

www.porte-voix.com/redgirl
D: benoit godde   C: benoit godde   P: benoit godde
A: redgirlz   M: redgirlz@porte-voix.com

www.pharmastar.it
D: gianluca campo   C: rudi oliva   P: medicalstar
A: energy   M: www.energycom.it

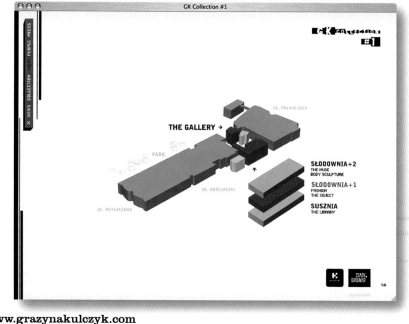

www.grazynakulczyk.com
D: arek romanski   C: lukasz knasiecki
A: huncwot   M: office@huncwot.com

www.irie.be
D: jan weiss   C: jan weiss
A: kreativkopf   M: yes@imin.de

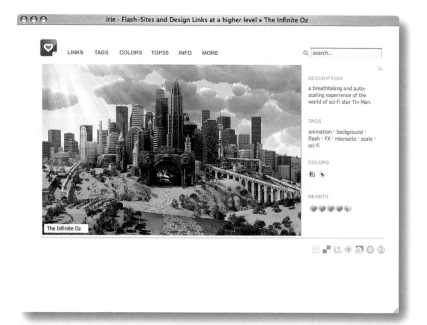

www.groomstudio.com.ar
D: diego pita, juan pablo segui, diego bercovich   C: juan pablo segui, diego pita
A: groom design studio   M: juanpablosegui@groomstudio.com.ar

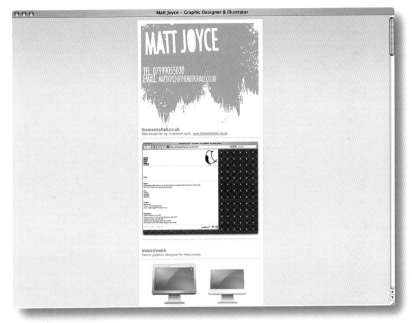

www.matt-joyce.com
D: matt joyce   C: matt joyce   P: matt joyce
A: matt joyce   M: mattjoyce@themeekshall.com

www.farmrio.com.br
D: seagulls fly team   C: seagulls fly team   P: seagulls fly team
A: farm   M: internet@farmrio.com.br

www.dresscodeny.com
D: andre andreev, g. dan covert   C: jon dacuag
A: dress code   M: casual@dresscodeny.com

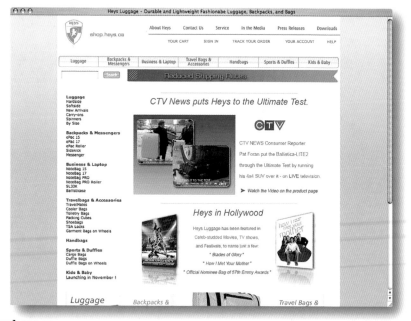

www.heys.ca

D: emran sheikh   P: emran sheikh
A: heys international. ltd.   M: emran.sheikh@heys.ca

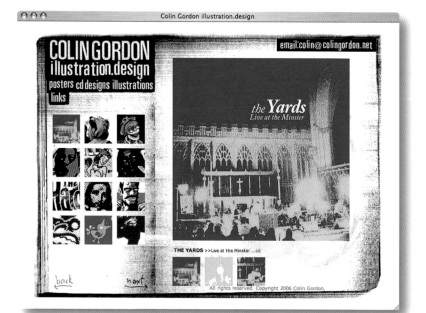

www.colingordon.net

D: colin gordon   C: colin gordon   P: colin gordon
A: colin gordon   M: colin@colingordon.net

www.cextema.org

D: bruno amorim   C: bruno amorim
M: geral@bruno-amorim.com

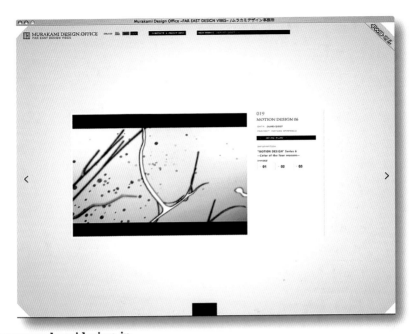

www.murakamidesign.jp
D: hidetsugu murakami
A: murakami design office   M: hidetsugu@murakamidesign.jp

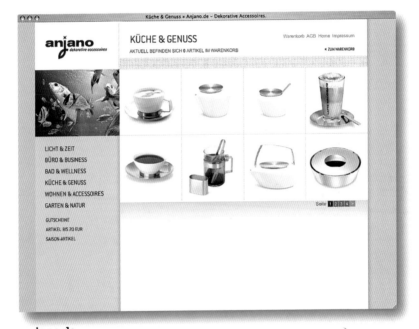

www.anjano.de
D: dennis rottler   C: volker schweizer   P: dennis rottler
A: cubus28 grafik   M: www.cubus28.de

www.zinkia.com
D: oscar garcia, hugo chacón   C: luis armengol   P: colman lópez, david cantolla
A: zinkia entertainment   M: host@zinkia.com

robert.dap.ro
D: robert pal   C: robert pal   P: robert pal
A: robert pal   M: robert.pal@gmail.com

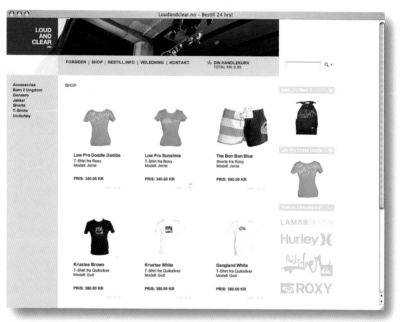

www.loudandclear.no
D: thomas orveland   C: israr khan   P: pagina as
A: pagina as   M: thomas@pagina.no

www.blublu.org
D: blu   C: blu   P: blu
M: notblu@gmail.com

www.matthewmahon.com

D: www.wefail.com   C: martin hughes, jordan stone
A: wefail, matthew mahon photo   M: martin@wefail.com

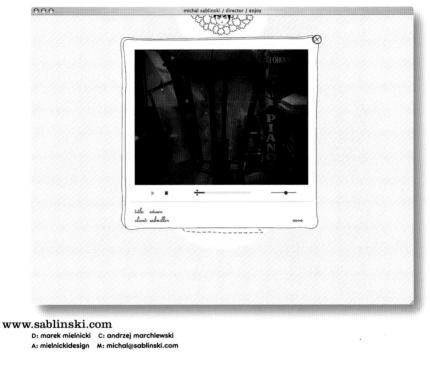

www.sablinski.com

D: marek mielnicki   C: andrzej marchlewski
A: mielnickidesign   M: michal@sablinski.com

www.alixlibert.com

D: alix libert   C: alix libert   P: alix libert
A: alix libert   M: info@alixlibert.com

www.wasmitmedien.de

D: malte müller

A: electricgecko   M: malte@electricgecko.de

www.roin.hu

D: robert szantai   C: robert szantai   P: robert szantai

A: roin   M: robert@roin.hu

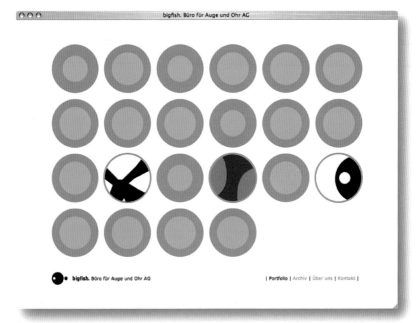

www.bigfish.ch

D: elke gülck   C: daniel meier   P: bigfish. büro für auge und ohr ag

A: bigfish. büro für auge und ohr ag   M: buero@bigfish.ch

www.webtoonfarm.com

D: paola infantino, caroline hue   C: caroline hue   P: dynamic foundry

A: dynamic foundry   M: info@webtoonfarm.com

works.wagnerpaula.com

D: wagner paula   C: wagner paula   P: wagner paula

A: wagner paula   M: wagner.nunes@gmail.com

www.kodacreative.com

D: david schoenecker

A: koda creative   M: info@kodacreative.com

www.designsul.pt
D: miguel gomes, fábio moreira   C: miguel gomes
A: designsul   M: www.designsul.pt

www.milligraph.net
D: emilie lebrun   C: emilie lebrun   P: emilie lebrun
A: milligraph   M: contact@milligraph.net

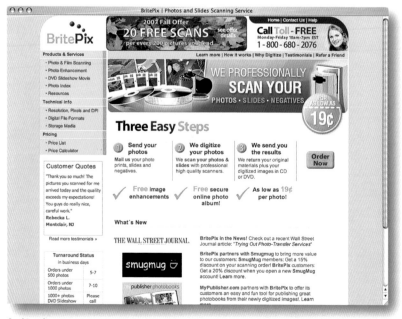

www.britepix.com
D: pablo barrantes   C: ricardo arce, marianela rojas   P: luis feinzaig
A: intergraphicdesigns   M: www.intergraphicdesigns.com

www.0717.at

D: lilo krebernik
A: 0717   M: hello@0717.at

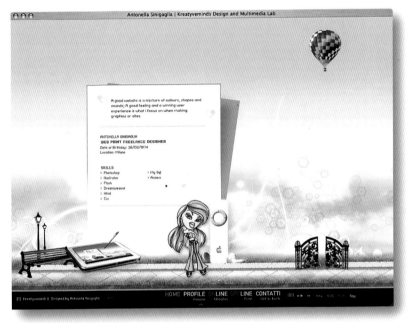

www.kreatyveminds.com

D: antonella sinigaglia   C: daniele cabrele   P: antonella sinigaglia
A: kreatyveminds   M: info@kreatyveminds.com

www.roughcutsmusic.com

D: matt bugeja   C: fabio zammit
A: bma ltd   M: info@bma.com.mt

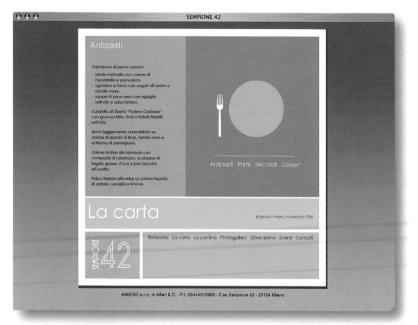

www.sempione42.com

D: manuela misani   C: manuela misani   P: paolo airaghi

A: ysg / isp   M: paolo_airaghi@fastwebnet.it

www.druiz.es

D: david ruiz rincón   C: david ruiz rincón

A: dosd comunicación   M: david@druiz.es

www.descience.ch

D: andrea ulrich, nadja stadelmann   C: andrea ulrich

A: descience   M: info@descience.ch

www.montealto.pt
D: pedro candeias **C:** pedro candeias **P:** pedro candeias
A: pedro candeias, architect I design **M:** mail@pedrocandeias.com

www.globalestates.es
D: global multimedia **C:** global multimedia **P:** global multimedia
A: global estates **M:** globalestates@gmail.com

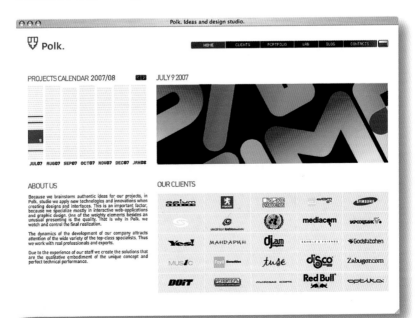

www.polkdesign.net
D: babich juriy, peter soloway **P:** babich juriy
A: polk. **M:** sales@polkdesign.net

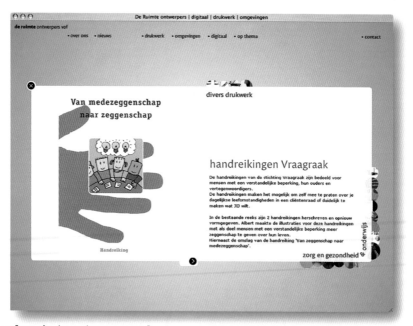

www.de-ruimte-ontwerpers.nl

D: robbert slotman, mark schalken, albert hennipman, bart heesink   C: bart heesink
A: de ruimte ontwerpers   M: info@de-ruimte-ontwerpers.nl

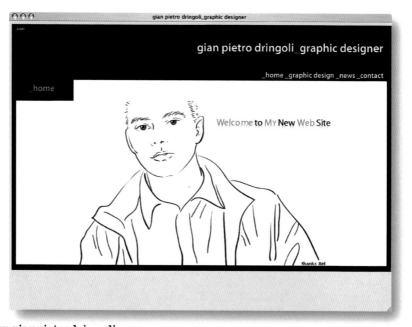

www.gianpietrodringoli.com

D: gian pietro dringoli   C: xel   P: gian pietro dringoli
A: gian pietro dringoli_graphic designer   M: info@gianpietrodringoli.com

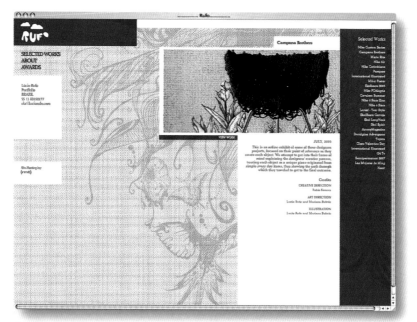

www.luciorufo.com

D: lucio rufo   C: andre brunetta   P: lucio rufo
A: lucio rufo   M: ola@luciorufo.com

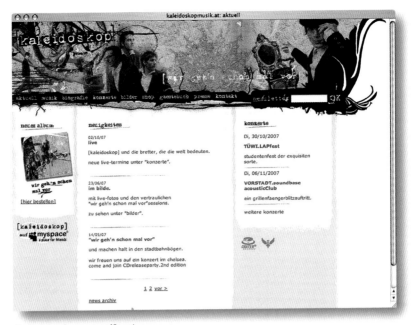

www.kaleidoskopmusik.at
D: michael zagorski, markus raffelsberger   C: klaus prochart   P: helmut prochart
A: sitedefinition, valence   M: www.sitedefinition.at

www.nipaz.com
D: norio ichikawa   C: norio ichikawa   P: michelle nguyen
A: urbtype   M: norio@urbtype.com

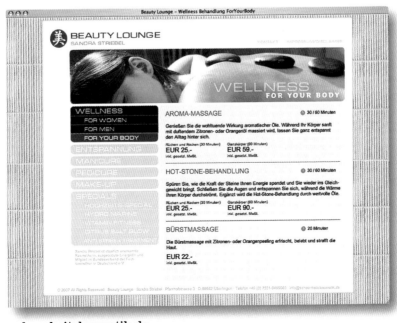

www.schoenheitskosmetik.de
D: stefan behringer   C: juergen wunderle
A: d:\sign creativeconcepts   M: www.dsign.de

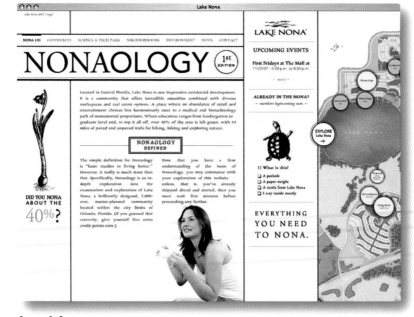

www.learnlakenona.com

D: ron boucher, mark unger, ian coyle   C: fl-2   P: steven marshall, ross bjork
A: push   M: munger@pushhere.com

www.letriojoubran.com

D: partikule studio   C: michel-ange kuntz   P: partikule studio
A: partikule studio   M: michelange@partikule.net

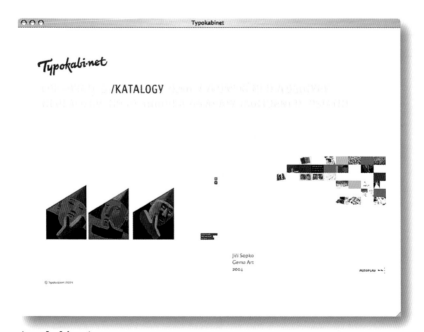

www.typokabi.net

D: michal smejkal   C: michal smejkal   P: michal smejkal, viktor beranek
A: typokabinet   M: michal@typokabi.net

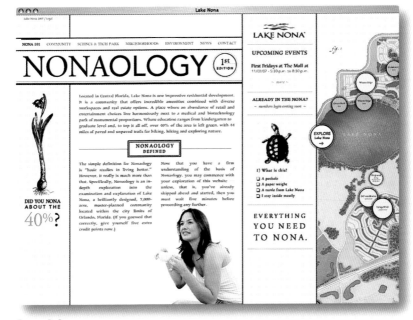

www.learnlakenona.com
D: ron boucher, mark unger, ian coyle   C: fl-2   P: steven marshall, ross bjork
A: push   M: munger@pushhere.com

www.letriojoubran.com
D: partikule studio   C: michel-ange kuntz   P: partikule studio
A: partikule studio   M: michelange@partikule.net

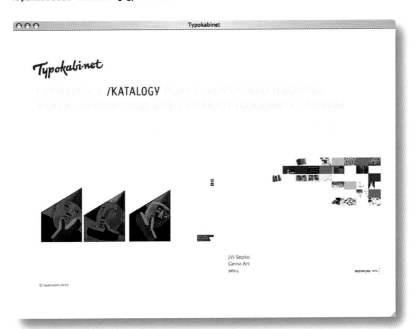

www.typokabi.net
D: michal smejkal   C: michal smejkal   P: michal smejkal, viktor beranek
A: typokabinet   M: michal@typokabi.net

www.whateverland.com
D: mark wisniowski   C: nazarin hamid   P: archie florcruz
A: whateverland   M: archie@whateverland.com

www.01importexport.net
D: dirk hoffmann   C: patrik de jong   P: patrik de jong
A: artificialduck studios   M: dh@01importexport.net

www.quietplease.net
D: tim jarvis   C: dan london   P: kleber design ltd.
A: kleber design ltd.   M: info@quietplease.it

137

www.popluv.com
D: felix ramos   C: felix ramos   P: felix ramos
A: popluv   M: info@popluv.com

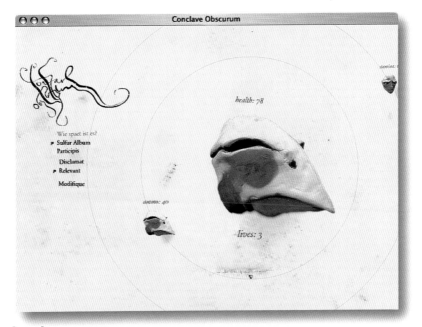

conclaveobscurum.ru
D: oleg paschenko   C: iv dembicky, oleg paschenko   P: oleg paschenko
A: art. lebedev studio   M: cmart@design.ru

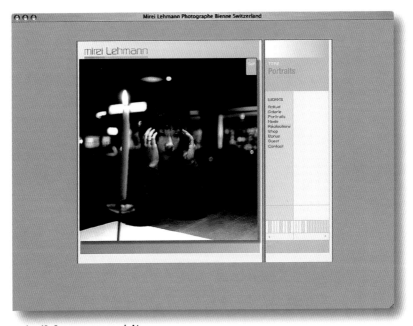

www.mireilehmann.com/site.asp
D: essence contemporary branding
M: info@mireilehmann.com

www.kaleidoskopmusik.at
D: michael zagorski, markus raffelsberger   C: klaus prochart   P: helmut prochart
A: sitedefinition, valence   M: www.sitedefinition.at

www.nipaz.com
D: norio ichikawa   C: norio ichikawa   P: michelle nguyen
A: urbtype   M: norio@urbtype.com

www.schoenheitskosmetik.de
D: stefan behringer   C: juergen wunderle
A: d:\sign creativeconcepts   M: www.dsign.de

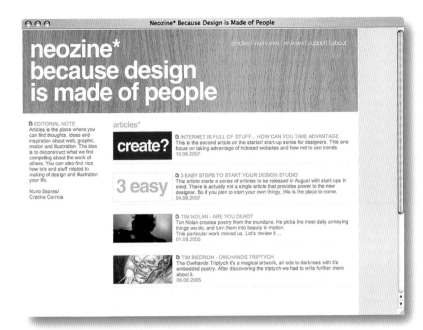

www.theneozine.com

D: nuno soares, cristina correia   C: nuno soares   P: nuno soares, cristina correia
A: nuno soares design - design interactivo   M: www.nsoares.com

www.lacoquette.com.ar

D: florencia fontana, agustina scaglia   P: hernan puente
A: visual box 1/1 studio   M: fontana.flor@gmail.com

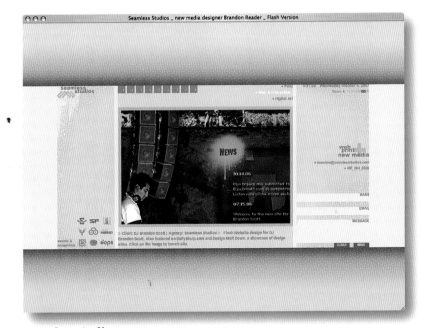

www.seamlessstudios.com

D: brandon reader   C: brandon reader
A: seamless studios   M: brandon@seamlessstudios.com

www.kylie.uk.com

D: antonella sinigaglia   C: daniele cabrele   P: antonella sinigaglia
A: kreatyveminds   M: info@kreatyveminds.com

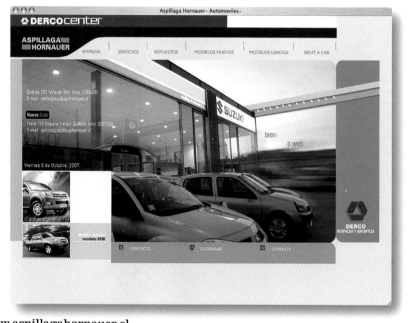

www.aspillagahornauer.cl

D: cristian salinas   C: cristian salinas   P: automotora aspillaga hornauer
A: csc   M: cristiandiseno@gmail.com

www.foundationpost.com

D: brian steckel   C: brian steckel   P: samantha hart
A: foundation content   M: samantha@foundationpost.com

www.riwalik.info

D: riwal plaine   C: riwal plaine   P: riwal plaine
A: riwal plaine   M: riwalik@gmail.com

www.3point5.be

D: pascal liénard, michael lhoir   C: pascal liénard   P: 3point5
A: 3point5   M: pascal@3point5.be

www.cameron-studio.com

D: cameron wilson   C: alaa-eddine mendili   P: cameron wilson
A: cameron studio   M: camerondesign@gmail.com

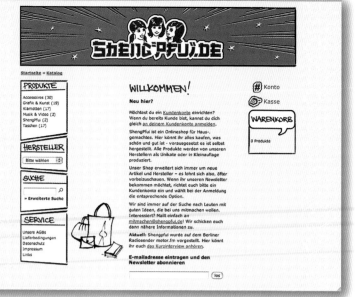

www.shengpfui.de
D: beate bolte, juliane strehmann, gesine todt   C: michael krenz   P: shengpfui
A: shengpfui   M: beate@shengpfui.de

odopod.com
D: curtis nishimura, joel francke   C: steve mason   P: kris smtih
A: odopod   M: stacy@odopod.com

www.bilateralstudio.com
D: diego mora, carla serena
A: bilateral studio   M: info@bilateralstudio.com

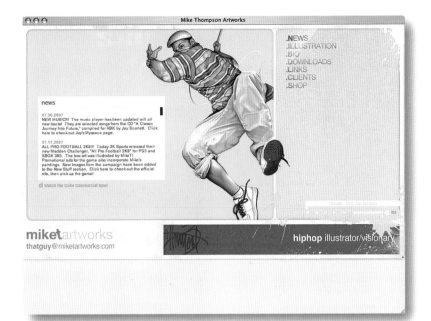

www.miketartworks.com

D: mike thompson   C: neopen studio

A: mike t artworks, llc.   M: thatguy@miketartworks.com

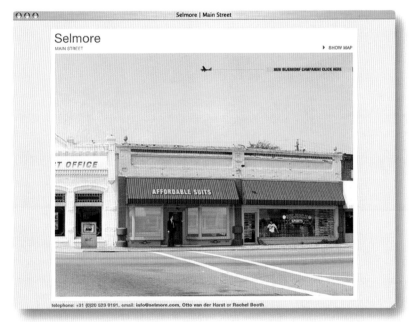

www.selmore.nl

D: pepijn zuijderwijk   C: joeri van oostveen

A: saltedherring   M: pep@saltedherring.com

www.kimm.no

D: kimm saatvedt, morten iveland   C: morten iveland

M: kimm@kimm.no

www.bunker.es
D: ragde   C: ragde   P: ragde
A: rgd creative concept   M: www.ragde.com

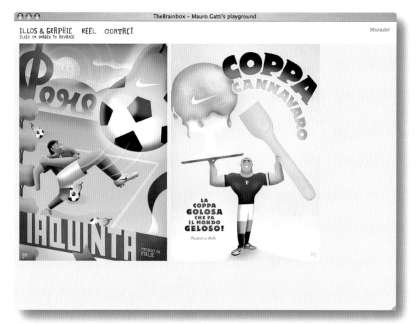

www.thebrainbox.com
D: mauro gatti   C: www.loadrevolver.com   P: mauro gatti
A: thebrainbox   M: mauro@thebrainbox.com

www.frauenaerzte-alzenau.de
D: claus roland heinrich   C: patricia prem   P: dr. sibylle kaßpohl, dr. andreas botschek
A: heinrichplusprem kommunikationsdesign salzburg   M: hallo@heinrichplusprem.com

www.avsd01.com
D: david godfrin, didier legrand
A: avsd01　M: versus@avsd10.com

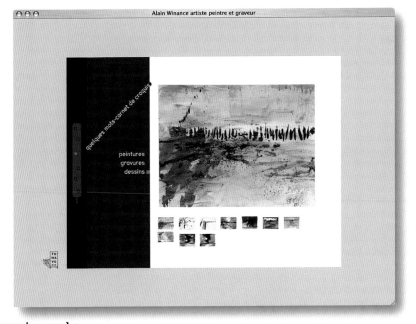

www.winance.be
D: pierre van de velde, sylvain bayart　C: pierre van de velde, sylvain bayart
A: tumavu　M: info@tumavu.biz

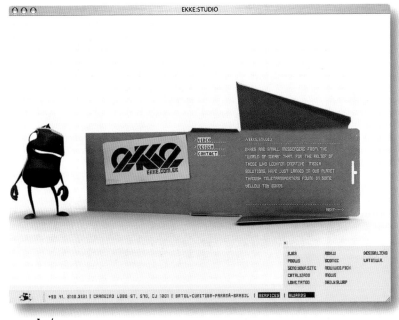

ekke.com.br/en
D: d.miguel, luciano berutti　C: d.miguel　P: d.miguel
A: ekke:studio　M: criacao@ekke.com.br

www.wellness-stars.de
D: mathias heinzler   C: christian miller   P: nextex medienagentur
A: nextex medienagentur   M: www.nextex.de

www.zaven.net
D: marco zavagno
A: zaven   M: info@zaven.net

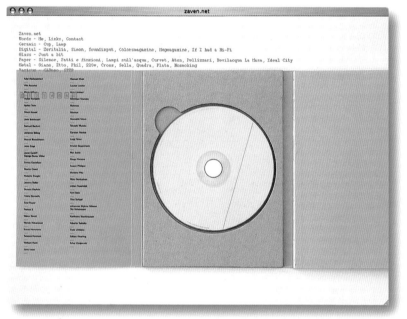

www.studiomonster.nl
D: boudewijn danser   C: chimedia
A: studio monster   M: bijtme@studiomonster.nl

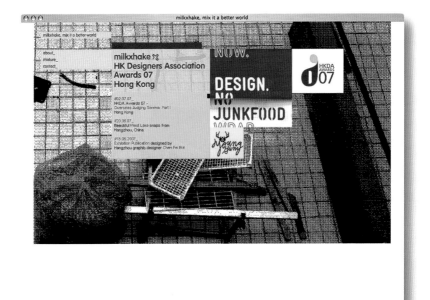

www.milkxhake.org
D: milkxhake
A: milkxhake   M: wilson@milkxhake.org

www.swallow.net.au
D: nelson mercadal   C: nelson mercadal   P: andrew rose
A: swallow creative   M: inquire@swallow.net.au

www.theapt.com
D: peter crnokrak, stefan boublil   C: method   P: the apartment
A: the apartment   M: stefan@theapt.com

www.caoz.com

D: magnus arason, magne kwam   C: samuel jonasson   P: hilmar sigurdsson
A: caoz ltd   M: hilmar@caoz.is

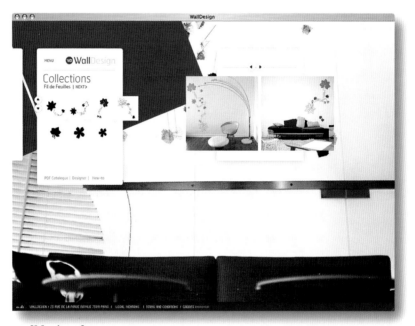

www.walldesign.fr

D: julien blanchet   C: guillaume delaballe   P: walldesign
A: rezo zero   M: contact@rezo-zero.com

www.usj19.com.my

D: alvin yap chun yu   C: alfred liew kim lim   P: deric leau
A: deleau creative studio   M: darcangel.alfred@gmail.com

www.funkypunky.ru
D: nikita obukhov aka greensun   C: nikita obukhov   P: nikita obukhov
A: funkypunky   M: greensun@mail.ru

www.staeheli.de
D: matthias staeheli   C: matthias staeheli   P: matthias staeheli
A: kotton designshirts   M: order@kotton.de

www.margotblanche.com
D: nick la   C: nick la
A: margot blanche music   M: management@margotblanche.com

www.ifva.com

D: john chan, ahman   C: anthony ng   P: postgal.com, pam hung
A: ifva   M: ifva@hkac.org.hk

sophiegriotto.com

D: sophie griotto
A: agent caroline marechal   M: caroline@caroline-marechal.fr

www.yopark.com.hk

D: john chan, siu san   C: anthony ng   P: postgal.com
A: yo park   M: postgal@gmail.com

www.surfaceview.co.uk
D: nb studio   C: engage studios   P: michael ayerst
A: surface view   M: info@surfaceview.co.uk

www.ovejanegra-producciones.cl
D: alvaro parrague ayala   C: alvaro parrague ayala   P: alvaro parrague ayala
A: netdesign   M: alvaro@netdesign.cl

www.koko3.fi
D: antti hinkula, teemu suviala   C: timo koro   P: syrup helsinki
A: syrup helsinki   M: koko3@koko3.fi

www.design-by-us.com

D: the design by us team   C: autocad, 3d studiomax, rhino, inventor   P: design by us
A: design by us   M: nicoline@design-by-us.com

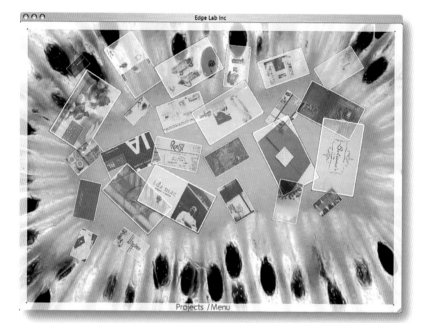

www.edgelabinc.com

D: alon zouaretz   C: alon zouaretz   P: lora appleton
A: edge lab   M: hello@edgelabinc.com

www.ventilatie.tv

D: ram broekaert
A: mediamind   M: www.mediamind.be

www.frekinglab.com
D: fredy lievano   C: fredy lievano   P: fredy lievano
A: frekinglab   M: fl@frekinglab.com

www.guillaume-rondet.fr
D: guillaume rondet   C: guillaume rondet   P: guillaume rondet
A: guillaume rondet   M: webmaster@guillaume-rondet.fr

www.artscode.com
D: fabio benedetti   C: fabio benedetti   P: fabio benedetti
A: artscode   M: info@artscode.com

www.gastoncaba.com.ar

D: gaston caba   C: nicolás cohen   P: gaston caba
A: gaston caba   M: www.gastoncaba.com.ar

www.airfix.com

D: pete vinnicombe   C: craig bovis
A: red ant   M: pete.vinnicombe@redantdesign.com

www.loungepenguin.co.uk

D: matt keogh   C: matt keogh   P: matt keogh
M: mattk@loungepenguin.co.uk

154

www.polyester.pl
D: jerzy michal dytkiewicz, lukasz wawrzenczyk   C: polyester studio
A: polyester studio   M: polyester@polyester.pl

www.linziehunter.co.uk
D: linzie hunter
M: linzie@linziehunter.co.uk

www.bomvol.com
D: born05   C: born05   P: born05
A: bol.com   M: rogier@born05.nl

www.ballettakademiepayer.de
D: marion waldmann   C: waldmann & weinold, kommunikationsdesign
A: waldmann & weinold, kommunikationsdesign   M: info@waldmann-weinold.de

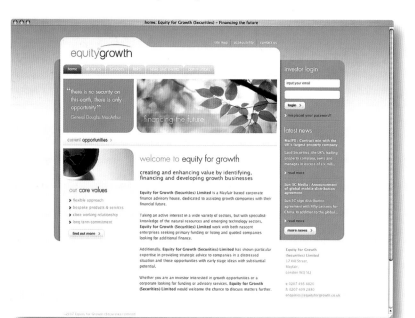

www.equityforgrowth.co.uk
D: trevor saint   C: trevor saint   P: trevor saint
A: equity for growth (securities) limited   M: hello@trevorsaint.com

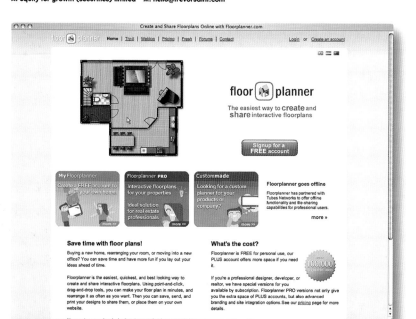

www.floorplanner.com
D: suite75   C: suite75   P: suite75
A: suite75   M: jeroenbekkers@gmail.com

www.kaeltetechnik-harrer.de
D: stefan behringer   C: juergen wunderle
A: d:\sign creativeconcepts   M: www.dsign.de

www.cuefusion.sg
D: cuefusion design   C: cuefusion design   P: cuefusion design
A: cuefusion design   M: www.cuefusion.sg/contact-us

www.pousadadocaju.com
D: luis kapinha, hugo vicente   C: hugo vicente   P: luis kapinha, hugo vicente
A: terradesign   M: kapinha@terradesign.pt

www.anjamedau.com
D: bert bräutigam C: iris breddin P: bert bräutigam
A: farbe M: hallo@farbe-form.net

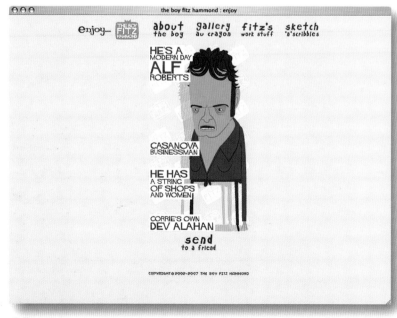

www.graphicaltravel.com
D: david verdier
M: hello@graphicaltravel.com

www.tbfh.com
D: the boy fitz hammond C: the boy fitz hammond P: the boy fitz hammond
A: the boy fitz hammond M: theboy@tbfh.com

www.mt-interactive.com
D: luc mauws   P: dirk tavernier
A: mauws & tavernier bvba   M: info@mt-interactive.com

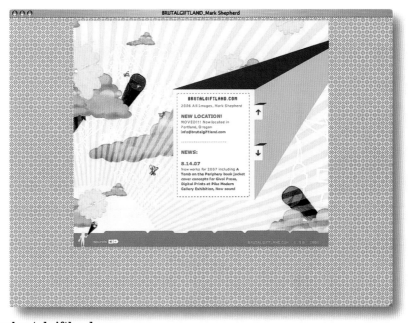

www.brutalgiftland.com
D: mark shepherd   C: mark shepherd   P: mark shepherd
A: brutalgift   M: mark@brutalgiftland.com

web.mytw.net
D: 朱政嘉   C: 朱政嘉
M: apig1403@yahoo.com.tw

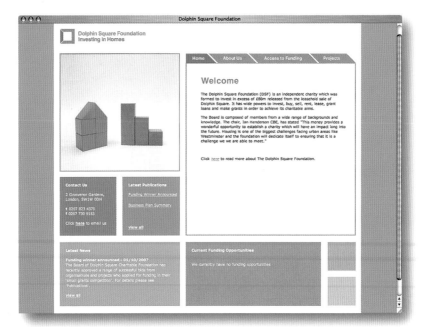

www.dolphinsquarefoundation.com
D: sam willard   C: sam willard   P: sam willard
A: 400 communications   M: design@400.co.uk

climaxdesigns.com
D: david blanchet   C: david blanchet   P: david blanchet
A: climaxdesigns   M: cd@climaxdesigns.com

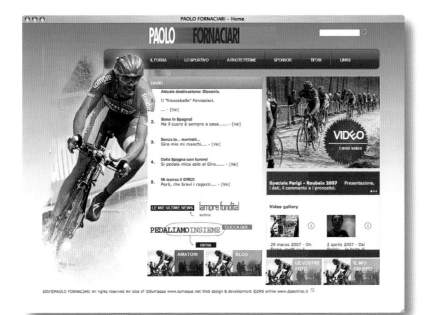

www.paolofornaciari.it
D: ilaria boz   C: maurizio albertoni
A: dps online   M: info@dpsonline.it

160

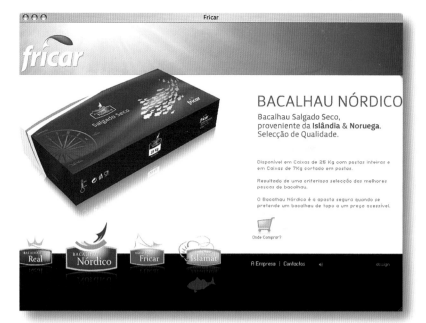

www.fricar.pt
D: adriano esteves, alexandre gomes   C: a. gomes, a. camacho, a. laurenço   P: bürocratik
A: bürocratik   M: info@burocratik.com

www.medicalstar.it
D: gianluca campo   C: gianluca campo   P: medicalstar
A: energy   M: www.energycom.it

wecreatethings.com
D: colin cameron, david blanchet   C: colin cameron, david blanchet
A: we create things   M: creatives@wecreatethings.com

www.lagencelibre.com
D: sokovision   C: benoit blanchard   P: eric marillet
A: sokovision   M: info@sokovision.com

www.jakestarwars.com
D: jake & tak! design and art direction   C: tak!   P: dom murphy @ tak!
A: www.taktak.net   M: www.jake-art.com

www.vidajovencr.org
D: ricardo arce   C: daniel obando
A: intergraphicdesigns   M: www.intergraphicdesigns.com

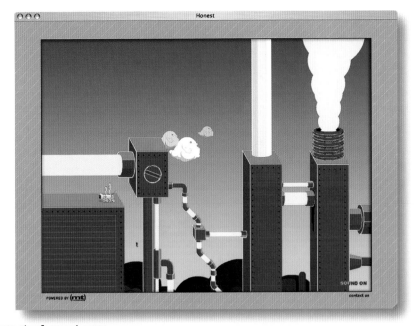

www.stayhonest.com

D: honest   C: honest   P: honest
A: honest   M: contact@stayhonest.com

www.bonsai-productions.de

D: florian müller   C: florian müller   P: florian müller
A: bonsai prod.   M: info@bonsai-productions.de

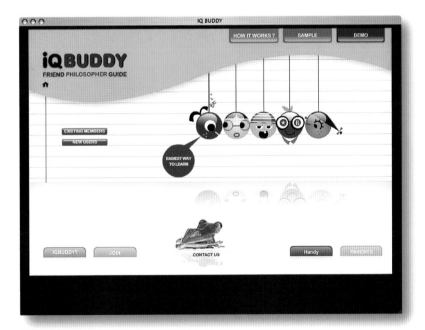

www.iqbuddy.com

D: candy singh   C: jaspreet singh   P: vishal gupta
A: magicmushroom.co.in   M: singhcandy@gmail.com

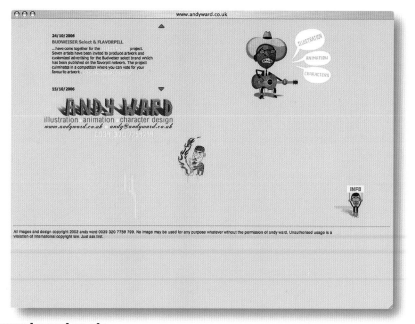

www.andyward.co.uk

D: andy ward   C: andy ward   P: andy ward
A: andy ward illustration   M: andy@andyward.co.uk

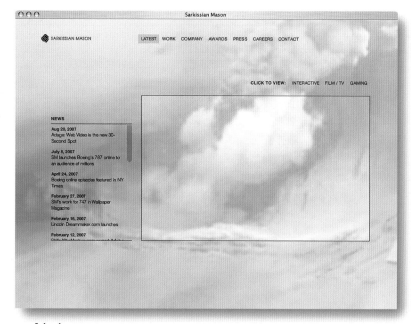

www.sarkissianmason.com

D: sarkissian mason
A: sarkissian mason   M: rp@sarkissianmason.com

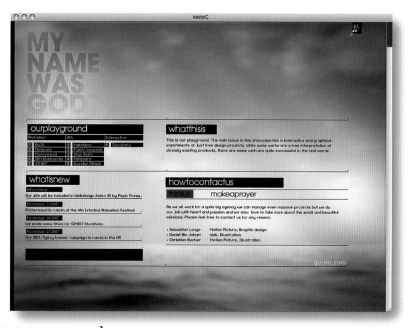

www.mynamewasgod.com

D: daniel bin johari, sebastian lange   C: daniel bin johari   P: d. b. johari, s. lange, c. bucher
A: qu-int.com   M: lange@mynamewasgod.com

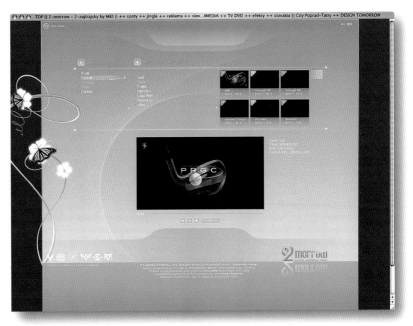

www.2-morrow.net

D: mio miroslav simko   C: mio miroslav simko   P: mio miroslav simko
A: 2-morrow, s.r.o.   M: mio23@2-morrow.net

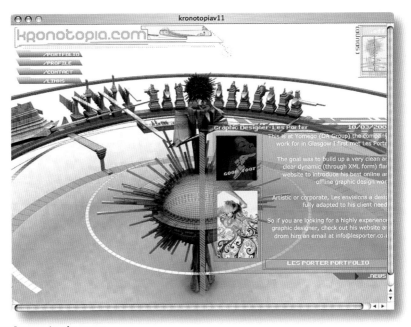

www.kronotopia.com

D: thomas barembaum   C: thomas barembaum   P: thomas barembaum
A: kronotopia   M: kronotopia@gmail.com

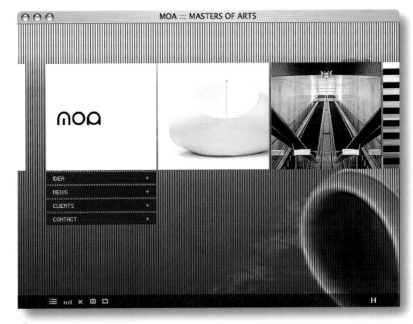

moa.pl

D: arek romanski   C: lukasz knasiecki
A: huncwot   M: office@huncwot.com

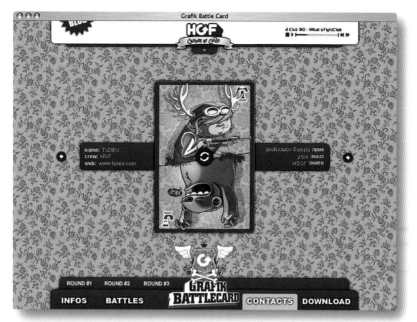

www.grafikbattlecard.com

D: sebousan   C: sebousan

A: jour   M: sebousan@gmail.com

www.bigyouth.fr

D: big youth design team   C: big youth programming team

A: big youth   M: contact@bigyouth.fr

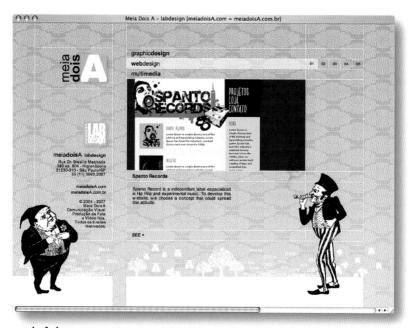

www.meiadoisa.com

D: eduardo soares, fabiola carvalho   C: eduardo soares   P: fabiola carvalho

A: meia dois a - labdesign   M: eduardo.soares@meiadoisa.com

www.skunky.it
D: riccardo pace
A: puffer design   M: riccardo@pufferdesign.com

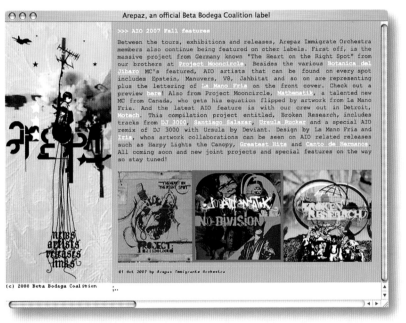

www.arepaz.com
D: la mano fria   C: gamebombing   P: beta bodega coalition
A: arepaz   M: info@betabodega.com

www.stfrancis.it
D: enza morello   C: lucas zanotto   P: st.francis design.communication
A: st.francis design.communication   M: enza.morello@stfrancis.it

www.bauer-lau.de
D: carsten tischer   C: jens richter   P: hofladen mathias lau
A: formschön werbeagenturen+tischer grafikbüro   M: kontakt@formschoen-agenturen.de

www.noisyyard.com
D: april chen   C: april chen   P: april chen
A: april chen   M: april@noisyyard.com

www.nateberkus.com
D: richard agerbeek   C: sweden unlimited   P: swedenunlimited.com
A: sweden unlimited   M: info@swedenunlimited.com

www.stellahernandez.com
D: miguel endara   C: miguel endara   P: stella hernandez
A: stella hernandez, photographer   M: www.stellahernandez.com

www.altimawebsystems.com
D: darya balova   C: vlad kolev   P: alexander levashov
A: altima web systems   M: www.altimawebsystems.com

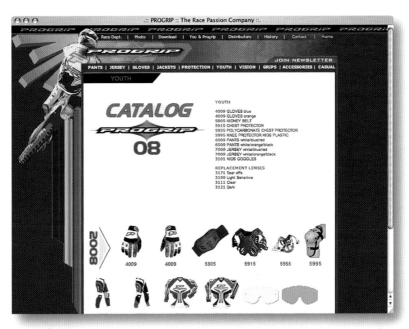

www.progrip.com
D: logical net srl   C: logical net srl   P: logical net srl
A: logical net srl   M: info@logicalnet.it

www.viva-consulting.ch

D: zoran bozanic   C: sabi cakiral   P: zoran bozanic
A: www.design-labor.ch   M: info@design-labor.ch

www.koendemuynck.com

D: group94   C: group94   P: koen demuynck
A: koen demuynck photography   M: info@koendemuynck.com

www.studiokowski.de

D: rasso hilber   C: rasso hilber   P: rasso hilber
A: nonverbla   M: rasso@nonverbla.de

www.pixelpastry.com
D: lim si ping   P: lim si ping
A: pixelpastry   M: ping@pixelpastry.com

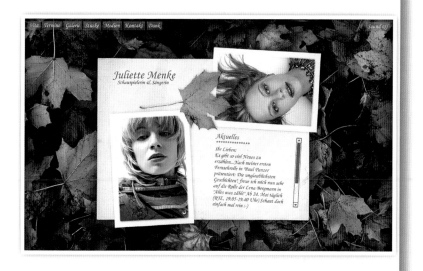

www.juliettemenke.de
D: christian grüner   C: christian grüner   P: christian grüner
A: pikestaff studios   M: post@juliettemenke.de

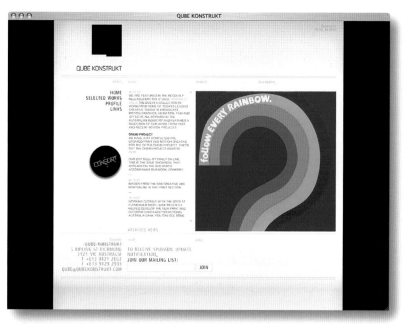

www.qubekonstrukt.com
D: qube konstrukt   C: qube konstrukt   P: qube konstrukt
A: qube konstrukt   M: sarah@qubekonstrukt.com

www.adrien-heury.net
D: heury adrien C: heury adrien P: heury adrien
A: heury adrien M: contact@adrien-heury.net

www.fubiz.net
D: guillaume allard P: romain colin
M: contact@fubiz.net

www.mdf.es
D: s.alonso, m.llorens, r.solano, s.estringana C: tiempo bbdo P: tiempo bbdo
A: mercado de fuencarral M: corinna@mdf.es

www.adrien-heury.net

D: heury adrien   C: heury adrien   P: heury adrien
A: heury adrien   M: contact@adrien-heury.net

www.fubiz.net

D: guillaume allard   P: romain colin
M: contact@fubiz.net

www.mdf.es

D: s.alonso, m.llorens, r.solano, s.estringana   C: tiempo bbdo   P: tiempo bbdo
A: mercado de fuencarral   M: corinna@mdf.es

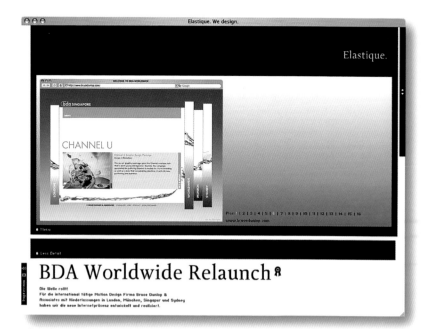

BDA Worldwide Relaunch ®

Die Welle rollt!
Für die international tätige Motion Design Firma Bruce Dunlop & Associates mit Niederlassungen in London, München, Singapur und Sydney haben wir die neue Internetpräsenz entwickelt und realisiert.

www.elastique.de

D: betty schimmelpfennig   C: karz von bonin   P: andreas schimmelpfennig
A: elastique. we design.   M: andreas@elastique.de

www.vosecretary.com

D: myroslav orshak   C: sergey lifinsky   P: yuriy semenov
A: mif design studio   M: www.mifdesign.com

www.arredogamma.com

D: andrea basile   C: basile advertising   P: andrea basile
A: basile advertising   M: info@basileadvertising.com

www.cocinashiperkit.es
D: toni sánchez   C: philipp keweloh   P: juan carlos rodriguez
A: probalear imagen y diseño s.l.   M: diseno@probalear.info

www.freakyfacets.com
D: johhny taylor   C: johhny taylor   P: johhny taylor
A: freakyfacets   M: johnny@freakyfacets.com

www.davidpintor.com
D: david pintor   C: carlos garcía   P: carlos garcía
A: isenda   M: davidpintor1975@yahoo.es

www.pixelpastry.com
D: lim si ping   P: lim si ping
A: pixelpastry   M: ping@pixelpastry.com

www.juliettemenke.de
D: christian grüner   C: christian grüner   P: christian grüner
A: pikestaff studios   M: post@juliettemenke.de

www.qubekonstrukt.com
D: qube konstrukt   C: qube konstrukt   P: qube konstrukt
A: qube konstrukt   M: sarah@qubekonstrukt.com

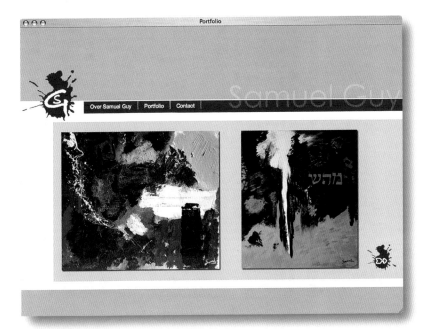

www.samuelguy.com
D: teun muusers C: teun muusers, peter meeuwsen P: teun muusers
A: vak18 M: info@vak18.com

www.recycledarea.co.uk
D: alberto seveso C: alberto seveso P: alberto seveso
M: albertoemiliano@recycledarea.co.uk

www.fonzietime.com
D: rui simões C: isac pinto P: rui simões, isac pinto
A: pixelstudio - soluções multimédia e internet M: info@pixelstudio.info

www.leecrum.com

D: lee crum, nessim higson, destin young   C: destin young, nessim higson   P: lee crum
A: lee crum photography inc.   M: lee@leecrum.com

www.alaripark.com

D: fabio de gregorio   C: luca milan   P: fabio de gregorio
A: drink creativity!   M: a.malgioglio@drinkcreativity.com

www.satchel-studio.com

D: kelty luber   C: kelty luber   P: kelty luber
A: satchel studio   M: kelty@satchel-studio.com

www.haveyouseenthisguy.com/photos
D: abhishek nimbalkar
M: abhishek@haveyouseenthisguy.com

d3zin3.net
D: danny teo   C: danny teo   P: danny teo
A: d3zin3.net   M: danny@d3zin3.net

www.netarena.pl
D: hubert swolkien
A: netarena - interactive agency   M: swolkien@netarena.pl

www.prosograf.com

D: daniel chicote   P: alberto chicote
A: proyecto y solución gráfica   M: estudio@prosograf.com

www.area3.net

D: chema longobardo, sebastian puiggrós   C: federico joselevich   P: area3
A: area3   M: barcelona@area3.net

www.xf-fx.de

D: christoph kowalski   C: christoph kowalski   P: christoph kowalski
A: christoph kowalski, future visual style   M: info@xf-fx.de

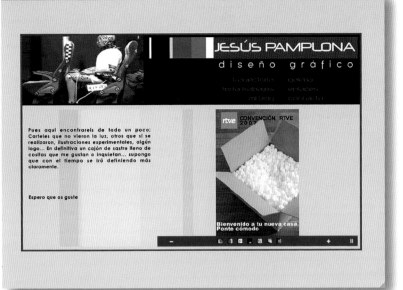

www.jesuspamplona.es
D: jesús pamplona   C: jesús pamplona, carlos sanz sayalero
M: cartaa@jesuspamplona.es

www.mixmedia.com
D: tracey lam   C: francis mak   P: jeremy lam
A: mixmedia production limited   M: www.mixmedia.com

www.nextideas.ca
D: jakub koter   C: jakub koter   P: jakub koter
A: next ideas   M: info@nextideas.ca

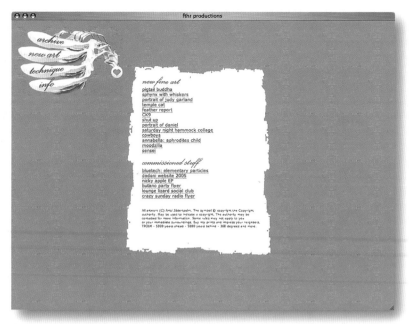

www.tpolm.com/fthr

D: fthr productions   C: fthr productions   P: fthr productions
A: fthr productions   M: fthrproductions@gmail.com

www.elizabethardenintervene.co.uk

D: martial boulguy   C: martial boulguy   P: elizabeth arden
A: internal studio   M: martial.boulguy@elizabetharden.com

www.neftysworld.com

D: neftali loria   C: neftali loria   P: neftali loria
A: my kinetic kreations   M: neftyloria@gmail.com

180

www.dedass.com
D: nik daughtry   C: step firth
A: ded associates   M: nik.daughtry@dedass.com

www.fabrikestudios.com
D: alejandro gonzález   C: alejandro gonzález   P: baobab producciones
A: baobab producciones   M: www.fabrikestudios.com

www.trelink.it
D: manuel dallolio, simone bellini, tommaso gavioli   C: antonio de luca   P: franca gori
A: tre intermedia network   M: mr.c@trelink.it

www.xoxii.com
D: suzanne marije cornelissen
M: suzannemarije@gmail.com

www.anevesefilhos.com
D: ana abreu
A: cores ao cubo   M: anabreu@coresaocubo.pt

www.aw-designs.de
D: wolfgang schröder   C: wolfgang schröder   P: wolfgang schröder
A: aw-designs   M: wolfgang@aw-designs.de

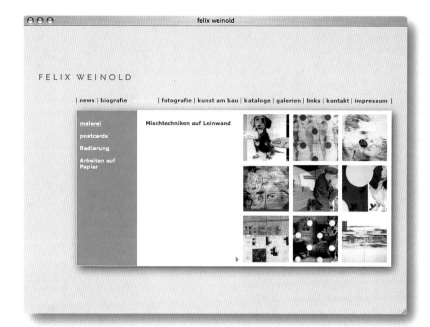

www.felixweinold.de

D: felix weinold   C: brigitte binder
A: waldmann & weinold i kommunikationsdesign   M: info@felixweinold.de

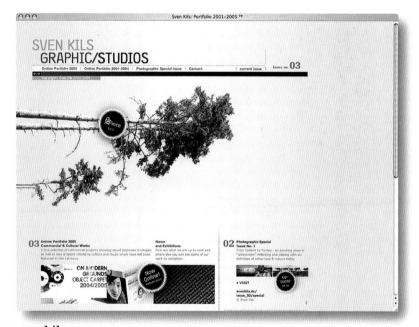

www.svenkils.com

D: sven kils
A: sven kils - graphic studios   M: info@svenkils.com

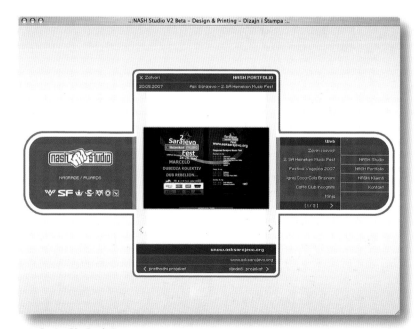

www.nashstudio.ba/v2

D: senad besirevic   C: nikola vujovic   P: nash studio
A: nash studio   M: info@nashstudio.ba

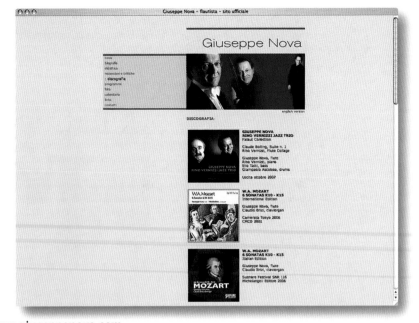

www.giuseppenova.com

D: ubyweb   C: ubyweb   P: ubyweb
A: ubyweb   M: www.ubyweb.com

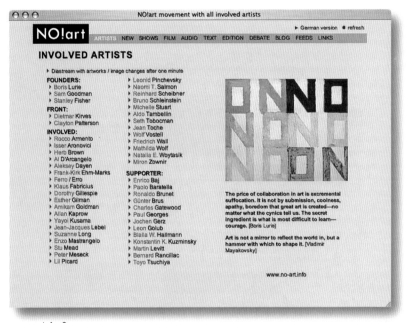

www.no-art.info

D: dietmar kirves   C: dietmar kirves   P: dietmar kirves, boris lurie
M: contact@no-art.info

www.inspiracionartificial.com

D: ricard rovira   C: miquel puig
A: inspiracionartificial   M: info@inspiracionartificial.com

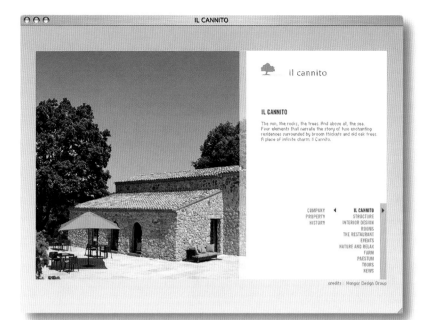

www.ilcannito.com

D: cristina bonaldo   C: barbara scalzotto   P: marina cabianca
A: hangar design group   M: hdg@hangar.it

www.calzadoscerra.com

D: adolo maragoto   C: miguel abal   P: juan luis hermo
A: dretec sl   M: info@dreitec.com

www.dotedesign.com

D: domenico tedone   C: pedro moraes   P: domenico tedone
A: domenico tedone design   M: domenico@dotedesign.com

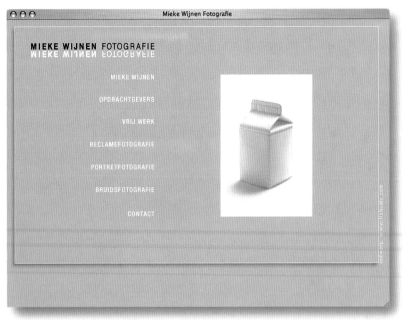

www.miekewijnenfotografie.nl
D: ellen groot roessink
A: www.fishuals.com   M: info@fishuals.com

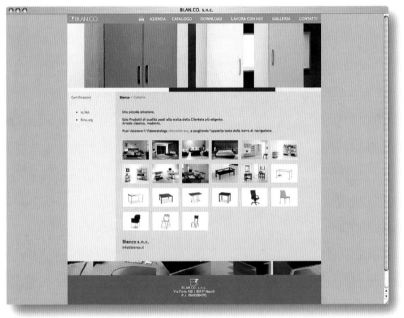

www.bianco.it
D: gabriele gargiulo   C: gabriele gargiulo   P: gabry gargiulo art director
A: gabry gargiulo   M: gabry@ondaline-adv.com

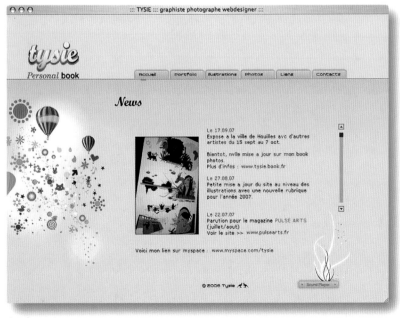

www.tysie.net
D: mohn damien
M: dam@tysie.net

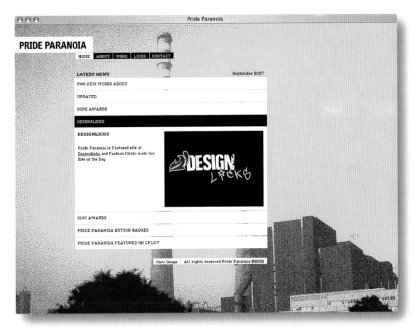

www.prideparanoia.com
D: joão planche   C: nuno ribeiro   P: joão planche
A: pride paranoia   M: jplanche@prideparanoia.com

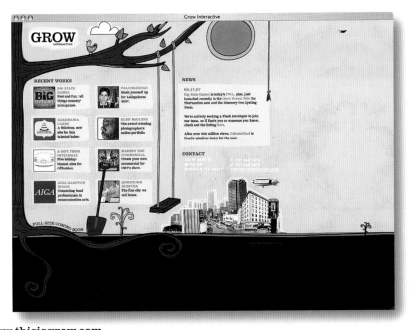

www.thisisgrow.com
D: joe branton   C: drew ungvarsky
A: grow interactive   M: info@thisisgrow.com

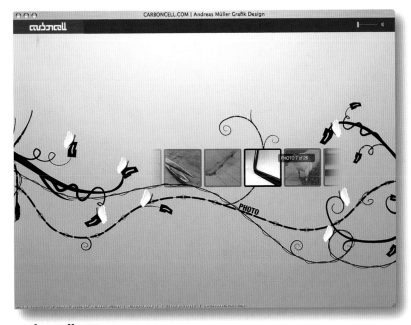

www.carboncell.com
D: andreas müller   C: andreas müller   P: andreas müller
M: info@carboncell.com

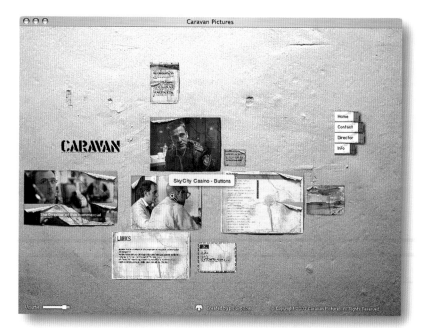

www.caravanpictures.com

D: henry chu   C: henry chu, anna tsang   P: henry chu
A: pill & pillow   M: welcome@caravanpictures.com

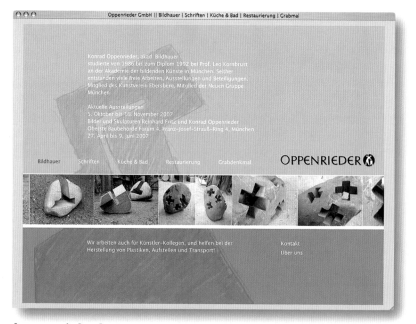

www.k-oppenrieder.de

D: kathrin demand dickmann   C: kathrin demand dickmann
A: blaupause   M: www.blaupause.com

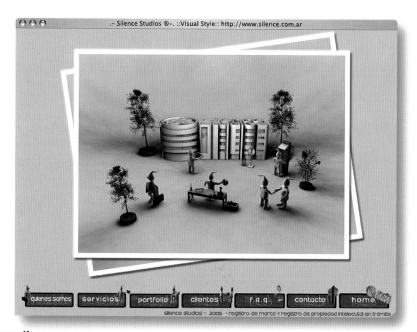

www.silence.com.ar

D: juan pablo dejean   C: ignacio dejean   P: juan pablo dejean
A: silence group argentina srl   M: info@silence.com.ar

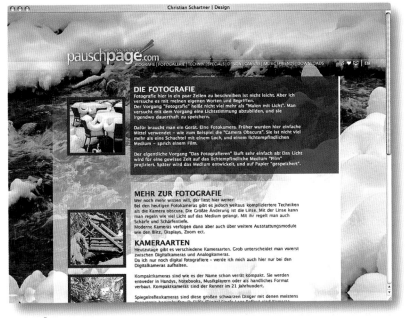

www.pauschpage.com
D: christian schartner   C: christian schartner   P: christian schartner
A: christian schartner   M: info@pauschpage.com

www.lo-fi.com.au
D: adrian guerin
A: lo-fi   M: adrian@lo-fi.com.au

www.spangemacher.com
D: vink pelicaric
A: rootylicious.com   M: office@spangemacher.com

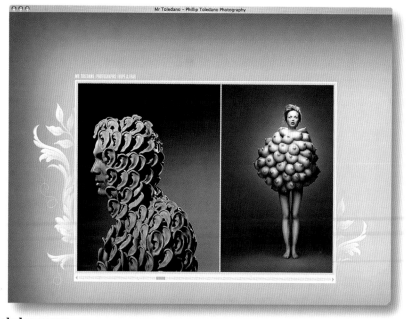

mrtoledano.com

D: nick felton
A: toledano photography   M: phi@mrtoledano.com

www.solar-company.com.pl

D: arek roma   C: arek roma   P: solar company ltd
A: solar comapny ltd   M: aleksandra.pyzio@solar-company.com.pl

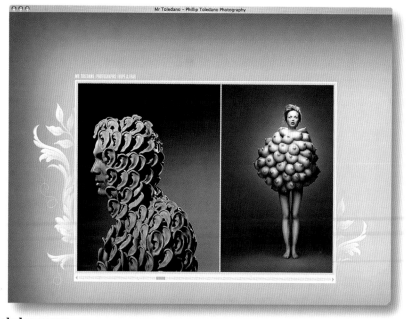

www.f6creations.com

D: fx. marciat   C: fx. marciat   P: xy area
A: www.xyarea.com   M: f6@f6creations.com

www.shoonyadesign.net
D: varshesh joshi   C: varshesh joshi   P: varshesh joshi
A: personal portfolio   M: varshesh@shoonyadesign.net

www.cubedesigners.com
D: jean françois castel, mathieu pesme   C: jens lofberg
A: cubedesigners   M: contact@cubedesigners.com

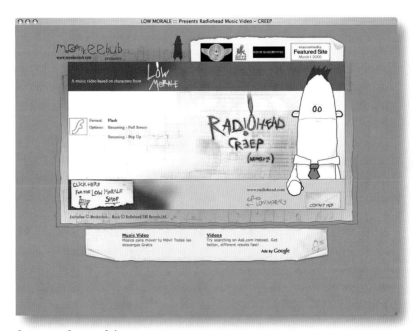

www.lowmorale.co.uk/creep
D: laith bahrani   C: laith bahrani   P: laith bahrani
A: monkeehub   M: lb@monkeehub.com

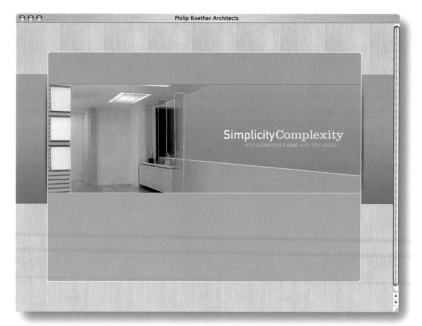

www.philipkoether.com

D: eric jordan

A: 2advanced studios   M: conatct@philipkoether.com

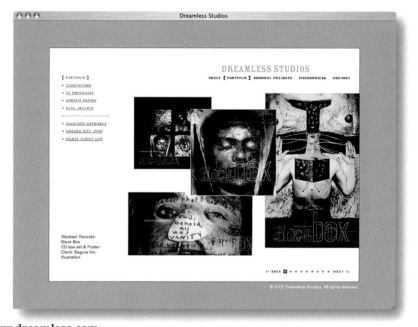

www.dreamless.com

D: eric dinyer, david decheser   C: adam coti   P: eric dinyer, david decheser

A: dreamless studios   M: dinyer@dreamless.com

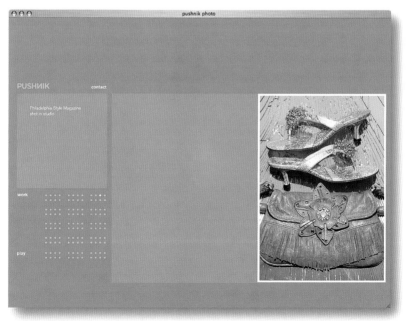

www.pushnik.net

D: flux labs

A: pushnik photography   M: pushnik@comcast.net

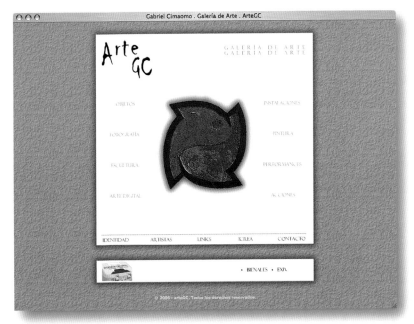

www.artegc.com.ar

D: silvina mones ruiz   C: silvina mones ruiz   P: silvina mones ruiz
A: silvina mones ruiz   M: silvinamr@gigared.com

www.textura-interiors.com

D: hunter
M: design@textura-interiors.com

www.layoutkungen.se

D: martin hultman   C: thomas krajewski   P: martin hultman
A: layoutkungen   M: martin@layoutkungen.se

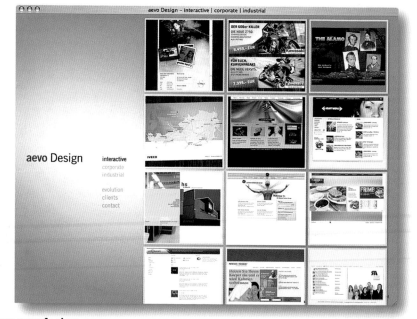

www.aevodesign.com
D: martin huber   C: markus lackner
A: aevo design   M: office@aevodesign.com

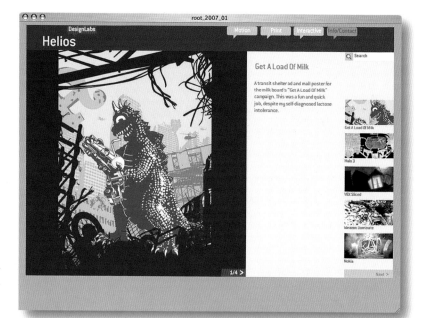

www.heliozilla.com
D: alex wittholz   C: mike robbins
A: helios design labs   M: hello@heliozilla.com

www.mundoaccesorio.cl
D: cristian salinas   C: cristian salinas   P: ma
A: cad4   M: cristiandiseno@gmail.com

www.kinetic.com.sg
D: sean lam   C: sean lam
A: kinetic singapore   M: sean@kinetic.com.sg

www.tanja-oberst.de
D: tanja oberst   C: tanja puls
M: info@tanja-oberst.de

www.fault151.com
D: mark sugdon   C: mark sugdon   P: mark sugdon
M: info@fault151.com

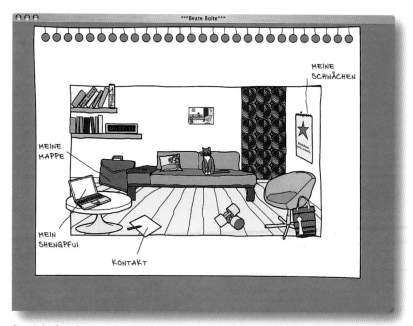

www.beatebolte.de
D: beate bolte   C: beate bolte   P: beate bolte
A: beate bolte   M: beate@shengpfui.de

www.artis.es
D: alt12O comunicació interactiva
M: contact@alt12O.com

www.bachritterburg.de
D: christian haas   C: christian haas   P: christian haas
A: nextex medienagentur   M: www.nextex.de

www.espace53.be

D: manythink   C: manythink   P: manythink
A: manythink   M: info@manythink.be

www.timeforcake.com

D: erin pheil   C: josh petrucci
A: timeforcake creative media, inc.   M: info@timeforcake.com

www.andersonoliveira.com.br

D: anderson oliveira   C: anderson oliveira   P: anderson oliveira
A: anderson oliveira   M: anderson@andersonoliveira.com.br

www.podol.cz

D: ondrej klos   C: ondrej klos   P: podol
A: podol   M: ondrej@podol.cz

www.azulvioleta.cl

D: pedro contreras v. - belgica cárdenas s.
M: peirocko@hotmail.com

www.gfdesign.art.br

D: gianfranco cagni   C: gianfranco cagni   P: gianfranco cagni
A: gfdesign.art.br   M: gfdesign@gmail.com

www.katjaschweiker.com
D: kai heuser   C: kai heuser   P: kai heuser, katja schweiker
A: heuserkampf - art direction for interactive media   M: cc@heuserkampf.com

www.cartonblanc.com
D: aurélien marcheguay
M: contact@cartonblanc.com

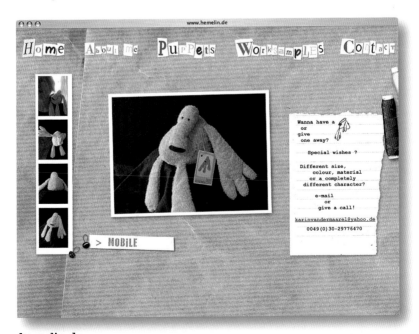

www.hemelin.de
D: mark van der maarel   C: mark van der maarel
M: m_v_d_m@yahoo.com

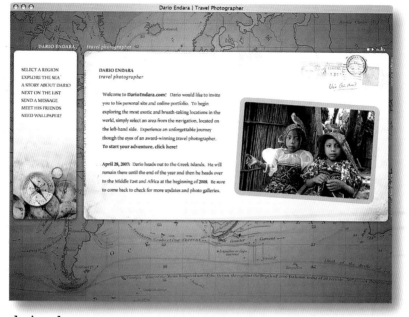

www.darioendara.com
D: miguel endara   C: miguel endara
M: dario.endara@gmail.com

www.romaingruner.com
D: romain gruner   P: romain gruner
A: romain gruner   M: info@romaingruner.com

www.petpunk.com
D: andrius kirvela, gediminas siaulys
A: petpunk   M: hello@petpunk.com

www.genuinephoto.co.uk
D: graeme swinton
M: www.graemeswinton.co.uk

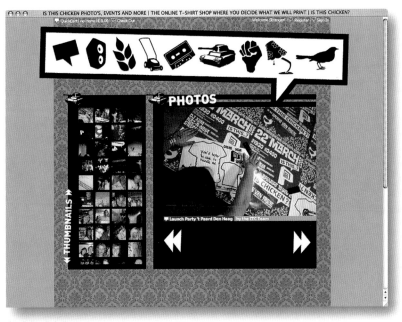

www.isthischicken.com
D: jilles sloos, tom boogerd   C: jerome bohg
A: is this chicken ?   M: info@isthischicken.com

www.jguevarra.com
D: chris peirantozzi, jacquelyn a. guevarra   C: chris peirantozzi   P: chris peirantozzi
M: www.jguevarra.com

www.berdber.com
D: josé casal   C: josé casal   P: josé casal
A: berdber studio   M: ze_casal@hotmail.com

www.umseisum.com
D: marta faustino   C: marta faustino, josé morango   P: marta faustino
A: www.martafaustino.com   M: www.martafaustino.com

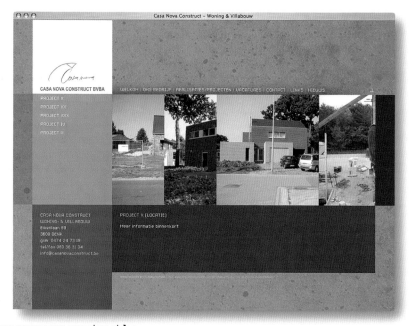

www.casanovaconstruct.be
D: kristof van rentergem   C: maarten bulckaen   P: kristof van rentergem
A: weblounge   M: www.weblounge.be

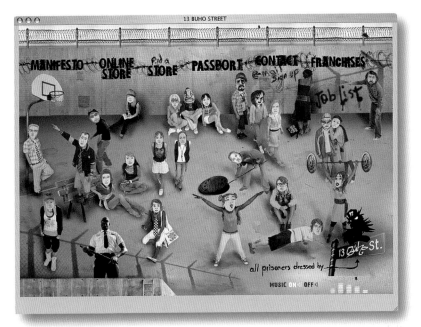

www.13buhostreet.com

D: 13 búho st. design team

A: 13 búho st.   M: expansion13@13buhost.com

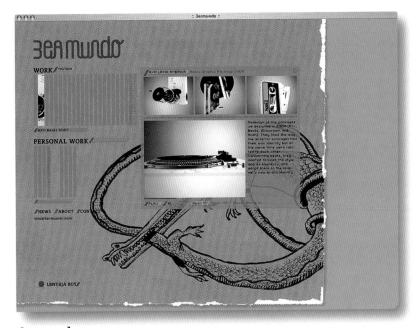

www.3ermundo.com

D: ramón parís, tere castillo, julia wolf   C: julia wolf   P: 3ermundo comunicaciones

A: 3ermundo comunicaciones   M: info@3ermundo.com

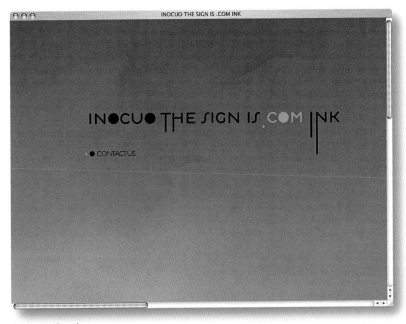

www.inocuothesign.com

D: javier gutierrez, david fernandez, txema alguacil   C: medusateam   P: miriam romero

A: inocuodesign sl   M: inocuo@inocuodesign.com

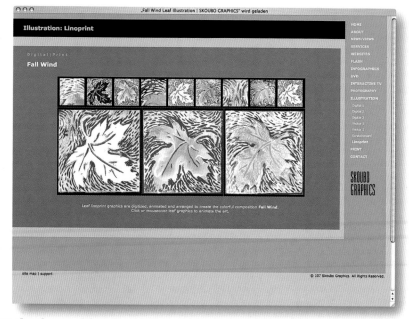

www.skoubographics.com

D: cher skoubo   C: cher skoubo   P: cher skoubo

A: skoubo graphics   M: skoubo@skoubographics.com

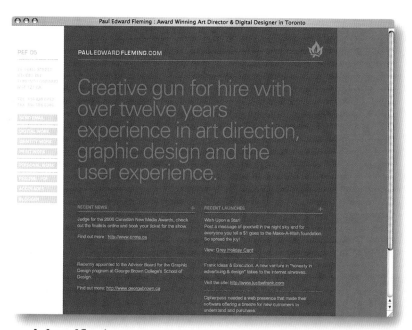

www.pauledwardfleming.com

D: paul edward fleming   C: paul edward fleming

M: paul@pauledwardfleming.com

www.trucker-mouth.com

D: tim atkins   C: tim atkins

A: walnut hill design   M: info@walnuthilldesign.com

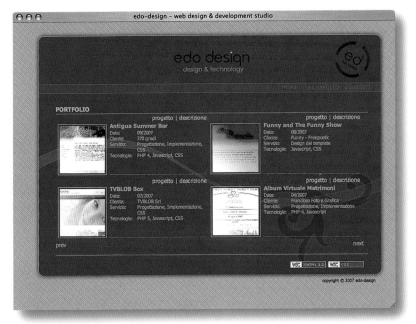

www.edo-design.com
D: edoardo esposito   C: edoardo esposito   P: edoardo esposito
A: edo-design studio   M: info@edo-design.com

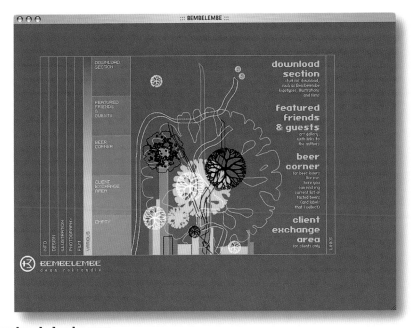

www.bembelembe.com
D: dean roksandic bembelembe   C: damjan krajacic   P: dean roksandic bembelembe
M: dean@bembelembe.com

www.bouncingorange.com
D: geraldine rey   C: geraldine rey   P: niek van santen
A: bouncing orange   M: www.bouncingorange.com

www.velcrodesign.com

D: pedro rebelo, davide silva   C: fernando marques
A: velcro graphic design   M: velcrodesign@velcrodesign.com

www.alexfernandino.com

D: mariana julião   C: mariana julião, philippe lima   P: mariana julião
A: alex fernandino   M: contato@maryjuliao.com.br

www.teladigital.pt

D: pedro dias   C: marco roberto
A: tela digital   M: info@teladigital.pt

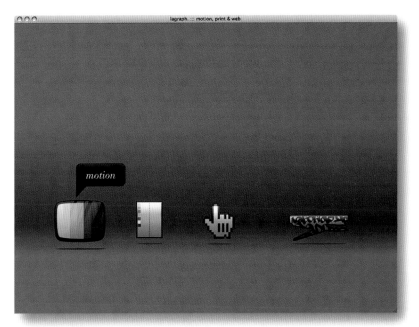

www.lagraph.net

D: hervé hiolle, pierre-adrien madec, xavier mathieu   C: xavier mathieu   P: h. hiolle, p.a. madec, x. mathieu
A: lagraph. [laboratoire graphique]   M: contact@lagraph.net

www.tempsgraphie.com

D: twistcube   P: isao naruse
A: twistcube   M: isao@tempsgraphie.com

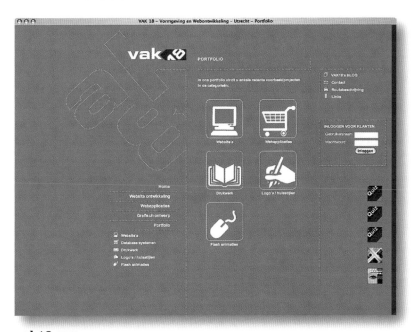

www.vak18.com

D: teun muusers   C: peter meeuwsen   P: teun muusers
A: vak18   M: info@vak18.com

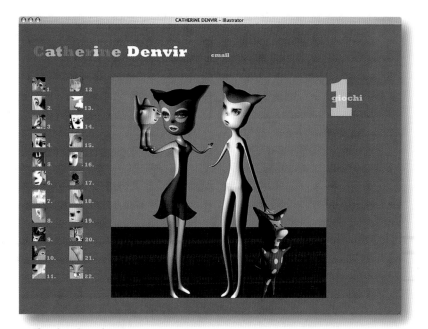

www.catherinedenvir.com

D: catherine denvir   C: george snow   P: george snow
A: catherine denvir   M: catherine@catherinedenvir.com

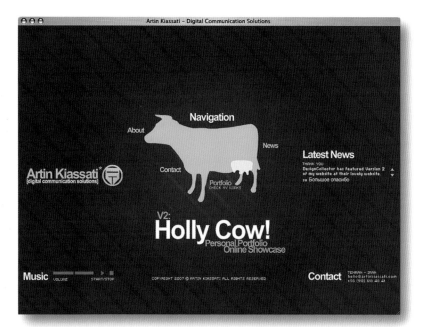

www.artinkiassati.com

D: artin kiassati
M: hello@artinkiassati.com

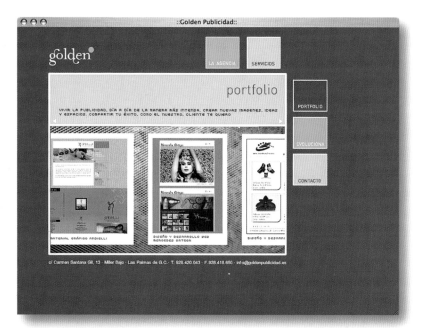

www.goldenpublicidad.es

D: golden   C: laura perez   P: iván ortega
A: golden   M: info@goldenpublicidad.es

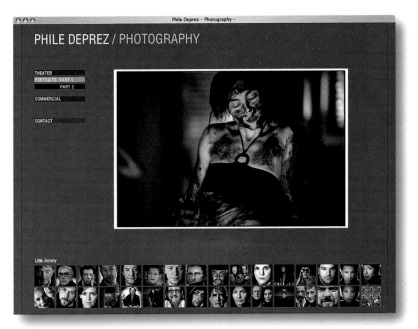

www.philedeprez.be
D: leen de smedt C: tim geyssens P: leen de smedt
A: ballyhoo webdesign M: info@ballyhoo.be

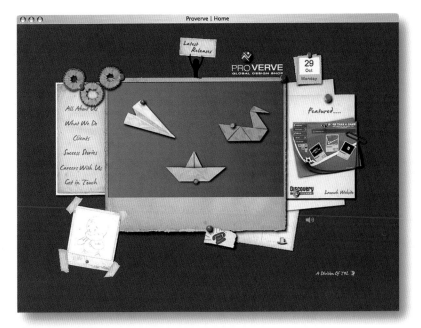

www.proverve.com
D: fahad moti khan C: bhushan verma
A: proverve | global design studio M: www.proverve.com

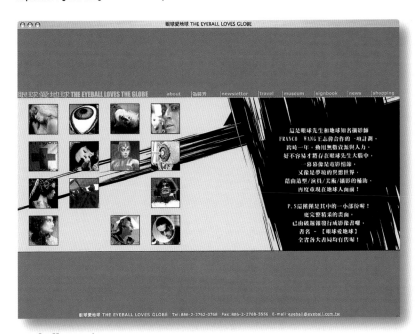

www.eyeball.com.tw
D: alice wu C: alice wu P: alice wu
A: the eyeball loves the globe M: dreamily5@gmail.com

www.schoonheidssalonambiance.nl
D: rémon van den bergh
A: remonvandenbergh.nl   M: info@remonvandenbergh.nl

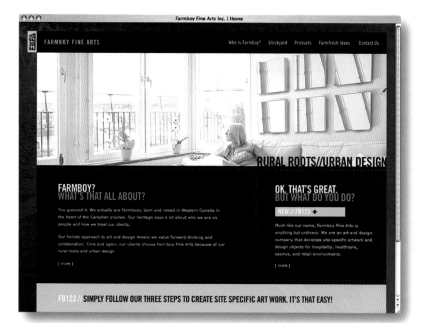

www.farmboyfinearts.com
D: peter figasinski   C: veratta   P: veratta
A: veratta   M: info@farmboyfinearts.com

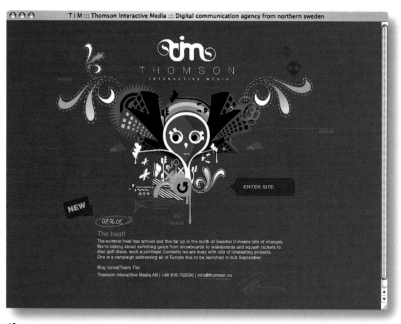

www.thomson.nu
D: thomas larsson, eric mårtensson   C: david sandström, kim eriksson   P: stefan thomson
A: thomson interactive media   M: stefan@thomson.nu

www.1000journals.com

D: brian singer
A: altitude associates   M: someguy@1000journals.com

www.punchkickinteractive.com

D: ryan unger, zak dabbas
A: punchkick interactive   M: info@punchkickinteractive.com

www.woerk.com

D: rasmus blaesbjerg   C: rasmus blaesbjerg   P: rasmus blaesbjerg
A: rasmus blaesbjerg   M: rasmus@woerk.com

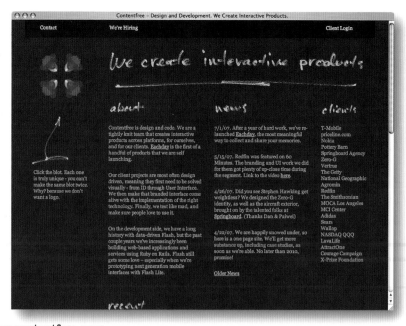

www.contentfree.com

D: trevor elliott   C: dave myron, william wong   P: trevor elliott
A: contentfree   M: trevor.elliott@contentfree.com

www.datoom.com

D: marcin krawczynski
M: marcin@datoom.com

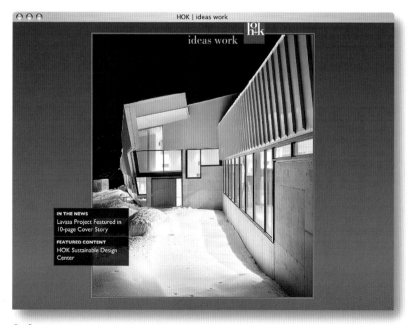

www.hok.com

D: toky branding + design   C: hok, toky   P: hok
A: hok   M: hokcontact@hok.com

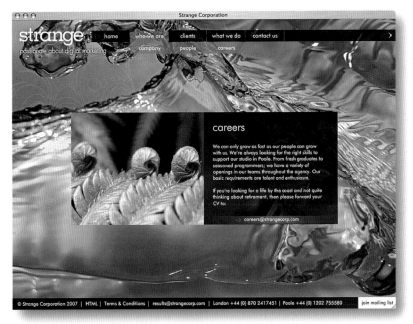

www.strangecorp.com/creative

D: jamie sergeant
A: strange   M: jamie@strangecorp.com

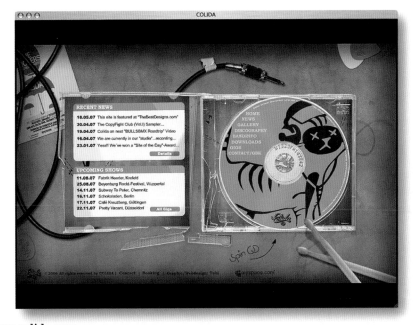

www.colida.com

D: tobias basan   C: tobias basan   P: colida
M: chopler@gmx.de

www.outwardcreative.com

D: eli horn
A: outwardcreative   M: elihorn@outwardcreative.com

www.patriciacorreia.com
D: ana abreu
A: cores ao cubo   M: anabreu@coresaocubo.pt

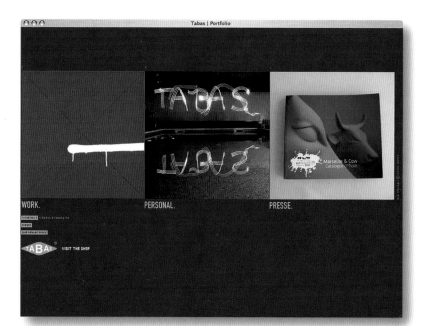

www.baseonebranding.co.uk
D: chris heron   C: sean higgins   P: paul hatcher
A: base one group   M: paul.hatcher@baseonegroup.co.uk

www.tabas.fr
D: cedric malo   C: tabas   P: tabas
A: tabas   M: cedric@tabas.fr

www.bnweiss.com
D: benjamin weiss   C: benjamin weiss   P: benjamin weiss
A: b.n.weiss | new york   M: www.bnweiss.com

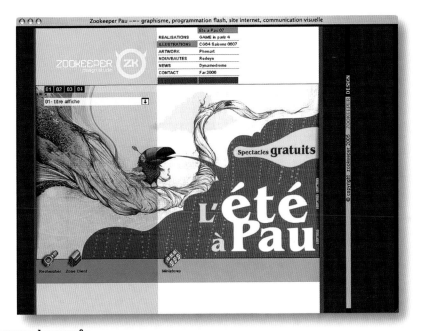

www.zookeeper.fr
D: dodzoo   C: moos   P: olivier ducuing
A: zookeeper   M: dod@zookeeper.fr

www.biffarmy.com
D: raquel agrella galván   C: raquel agrella galván   P: raquel agrella galván
A: rnroutlaw.com   M: info@rnroutlaw.com

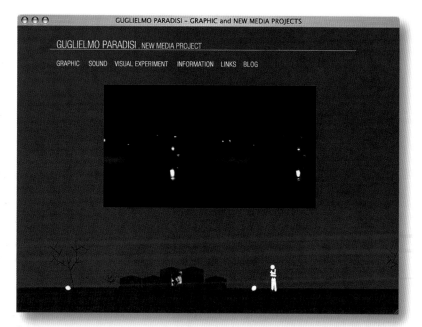

www.brainsworks.com
D: guglielmo paradisi C: guglielmo paradisi P: guglielmo paradisi
A: moti concept M: www.moti.li

www.esdesignusa.com/webdesign
D: elisa stambouli
A: es design usa M: stambouli@gmail.com

www.blende.ch
D: verena jung C: verena jung P: carolina piasecki
A: v2 M: foto@blende.ch

www.foccaland.com/2007

D: marcos paulo (focca)
M: marcospaullo@gmail.com

www.mattstuart.com

D: dominic geargeoura
A: loopdream.com   M: matt@mattstuart.com

www.taylorandbaines.co.uk

D: keiran anderson   C: tom cahalan
A: coding monkeys ltd   M: tom@codingmonkeys.co.uk

www.skwak.com

D: skwak

A: skwak   M: skwak@skwak.com

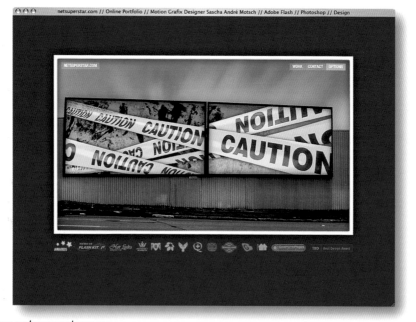

www.netsuperstar.com

D: sascha andré lanninger   C: sascha andré lanninger   P: sascha andré lanninger

A: netsuperstar.com   M: sascha@netsuperstar.com

www.danieladelforte.com

D: orietta verdiani   C: giuseppe tongiani   P: daniela del forte

A: confinigrafici   M: www.confinigrafici.it

www.leaopinto.com
D: bruno amorim   C: bruno amorim
M: geral@bruno-amorim.com

www.zee.com.br
D: fábio sasso, fabiano meneghetti   C: fábio sasso
A: zee - irrezeestível design digital   M: zee@zee.com.br

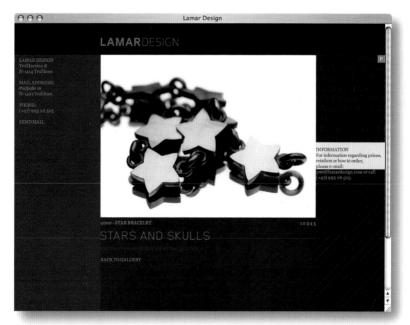

www.lamardesign.com
D: thomas orveland   C: thomas orveland   P: pagina as
A: pagina as   M: thomas@pagina.no

www.stephenbliss.com
D: stephen bliss, futaba hayashi   C: futaba hayashi   P: futaba hayashi
A: steroid   M: hellostephenbliss@gmail.com

www.if.net.my
D: liew sanyen   C: liew sanyen   P: christopher koh
A: (if) interactive   M: sanyen@if.net.my

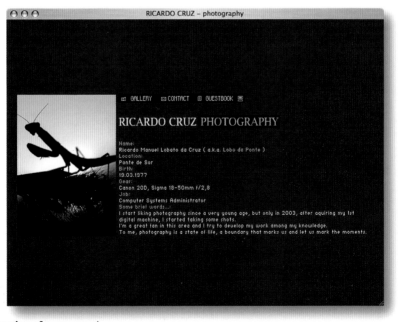

www.ricardo-cruz.net
D: pedromau   C: pedromau   P: pedromau
A: bad thiseyenz   M: pedromau@hotmail.com

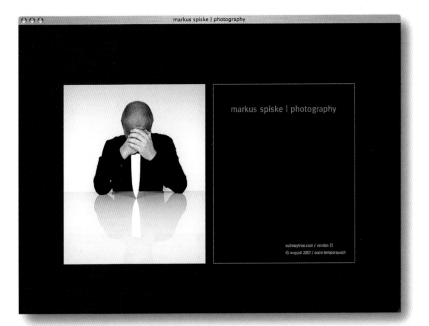

www.subwaytree.com

D: markus spiske   C: markus spiske   P: markus spiske
A: temporausch - kommunikation   M: info@subwaytree.com

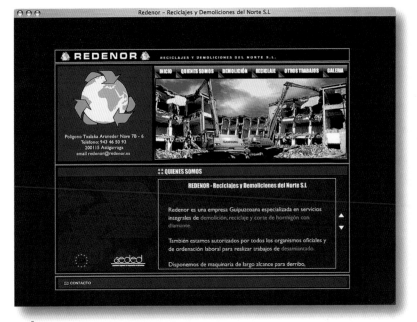

www.redenor.es

D: jon gonzález de amezúa   C: jon gonzález de amezúa   P: demoliciones redenor
A: amegraf   M: contacto@amegraf.com

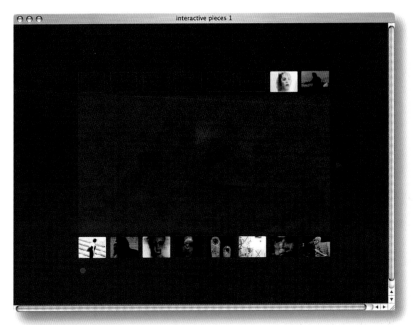

www.flyingpuppet.com

D: nicolas clauss   C: nicolas clauss   P: nicolas clauss
M: niclauss@flyingpuppet.com

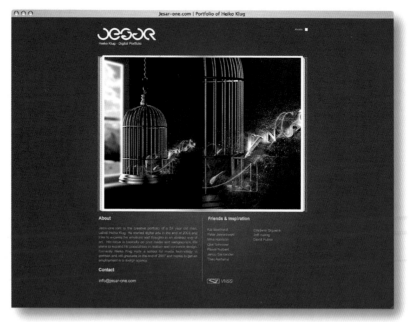

www.jesar-one.com
D: heiko klug
M: info@jesar-one.com

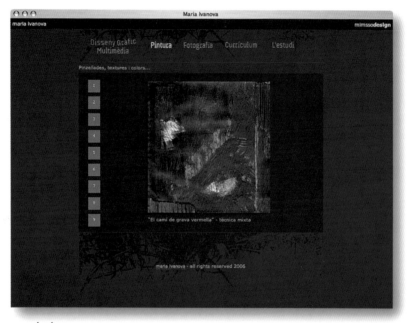

www.maria-ivanova.com
D: maria ivanova   C: maria ivanova   P: maria ivanova
A: maria ivanova   M: mimsso@gmail.com

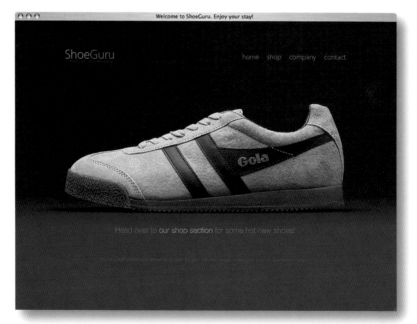

www.shoeguru.ca
D: yura sklyar   C: yura sklyar   P: yura sklyar
A: 350 designs   M: tom@shoeguru.ca

www.wideshot.be
D: didier legrand
A: avsd01   M: versus@avsd10.com

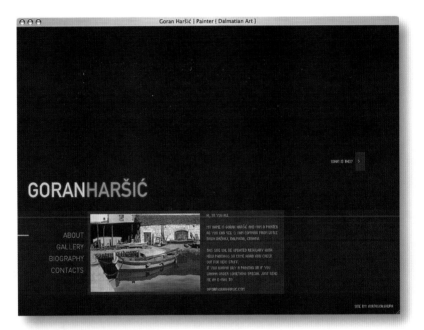

www.goranharsic.com
D: marko bjedov, mirjana batinic   C: marko bjedov   P: marko bjedov
A: atrtuska.grupa   M: desinner@atrtuska.com

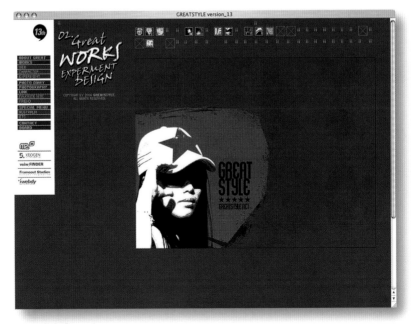

www.greatstyle.net
D: eom seung ho
M: greatstyle@naver.com

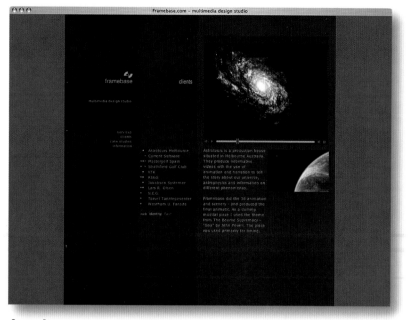

www.framebase.com

D: gunder bruun eriksen   C: gunder bruun eriksen   P: gunder bruun eriksen
A: framebase   M: gunder@framebase.com

www.henning-von-berg.com

D: christoph rietz, marco pflanze   C: christoph rietz, marco pflanze   P: henning von berg
A: mp-media   M: info@mp-media.net

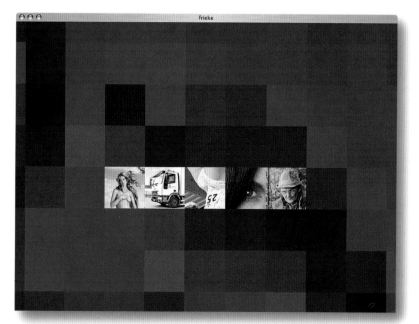

www.frieke.com

D: pure communication
A: miss frieke   M: mail@frieke.com

www.mushroom.es

D: andrés sparti   C: andrés sparti   P: guillermina trejo, luis delgado
A: the mushroom company production services   M: info@mushroom.es

www.claracollins.com

D: pierrick calvez
A: clara collins, tribulations   M: clara@claracollins.com

www.perspex.be

D: mathieu michaux   C: mathieu michaux
A: prspx // graphical propaganda   M: mathieu@perspex.be

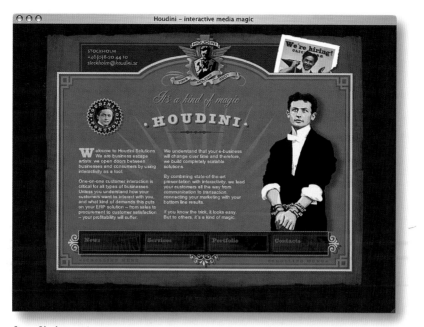

www.houdinigroup.com

D: jay sojdelius   C: johan lavenius   P: andré gottfridsson
A: houdini group ab   M: jay@houdinigroup.com

www.evolved.pl

D: kacper spala   C: kacper spala   P: kacper spala
A: qobdop   M: kacper.spala@evolved.pl

www.culti.ch

D: zoran bozanic   C: christoph adelmann   P: zoran bozanic
A: www.design-labor.ch   M: info@design-labor.ch

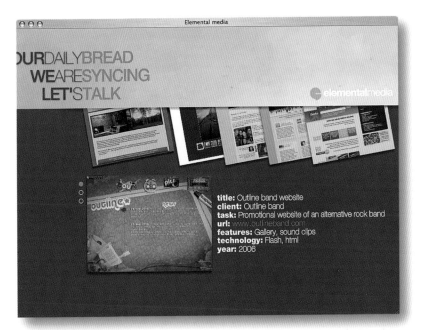

www.elementalmedia.info
D: stevo kralovic   P: stanislav majerski
A: elemental media   M: tomas@elemental.sk

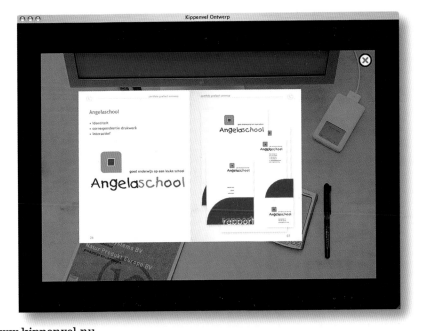

www.kippenvel.nu
D: roeland heesbeen   C: mark elissen (lab076)   P: roeland heesbeen
A: kippenvel ontwerp   M: ontwerp@kippenvel.nu

www.zen-studio.com
D: wide
M: contact@zen-studio.com

www.joaopedrocanhenha.com
D: joao pedro canhenha   C: joao pedro canhenha   P: joao pedro canhenha
A: joao pedro canhenha   M: info@joaopedrocanhenha.com

gregcrossley.com
D: greg crossley, freddy gomez. amin torres   C: freddy gomez   P: amin torres
A: univerzoo   M: gregcrossley.com

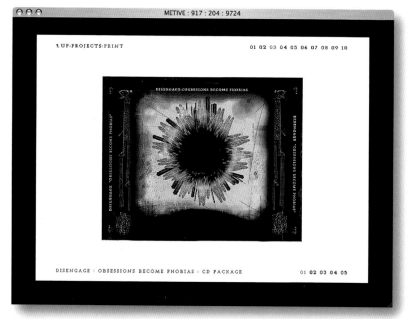

www.metive.com
D: robot01   C: robot02   P: robot03
A: metive   M: johnathan@metive.com

markgervais.com

D: mark gervais   C: mark gervais
M: contact@markgervais.com

z8.hu

D: krisztian puska
M: pyx@z8.hu

www.ibermaxi.com

D: pedro candeias   C: pedro candeias   P: pedro candeias
A: pedro candeias, architect I design   M: mail@pedrocandeias.com

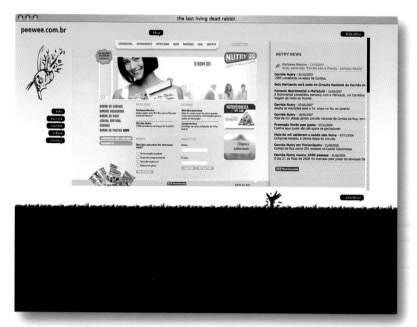

www.peewee.com.br
D: peewee   C: peewee   P: peewee
A: peewee.com.br   M: eu@peewee.com.br

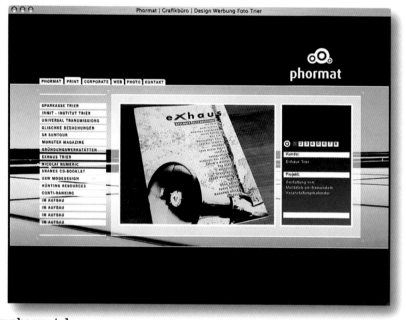

www.phormat.de
D: a. goltz   C: a.goltz   P: a.goltz
A: phormat.de   M: goltz@phormat.de

www.henrikbulow.com
D: kristian grove møller   C: felix nielsen
A: kriss créol   M: kgm@krisscreol.com

dan.vuletici.com

D: dan vuletici   C: dan vuletici, catalin saveanu
A: personal   M: dan_vuletici@yahoo.co.uk

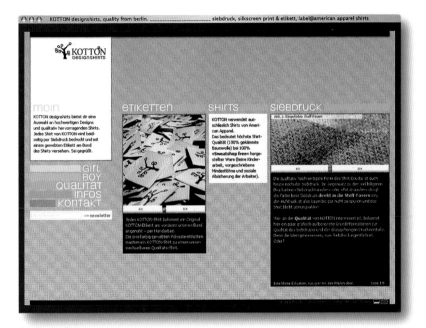

www.kotton.de

D: matthias staeheli   C: matthias staeheli   P: matthias staeheli
A: kotton designshirts   M: order@kotton.de

www.bravosite.tv

D: juan caballé, marcos girado   C: gustavo strassburger   P: juan caballé, marcos girado
A: bravo   M: rina@bravosite.tv

www.elyron.it
D: roberto balocco, roberto necco, lorenzo richiardi   C: lorenzo richiardi   P: elyron
A: elyron   M: elyron@elyron.it

www.jimherrington.com
D: jim herrington, ty lettau, frank ullenberg   C: ty lettau
A: jim herrington   M: jim@jimherrington.com

www.gugusland.org
D: thierry gaubert, emmanuelle barge   C: thierry gaubert
A: gugusland   M: info@gugusland.org

www.filippasmedhagensund.com

D: hugo ahlberg   C: eduard prats molner   P: mocoro
A: mocoro   M: info@mocoro.com

www.hmtmx.com

D: chi chau lam   C: chi chau lam   P: chi chau lam
A: cO6studio   M: info@cO6studio.com

www.tomter.net

D: sennep
M: jorn@tomter.net

www.sapien.com.br

D: santana dardot, gustavo timponi   C: sapien team

A: sapien   M: santana@sapien.com.br

www.hybride.com

D: jean-francois lemay   C: pascal rousse   P: bungastudio

A: kawabunga   M: sylvie@hybride.com

www.loftlinx.at

D: dietmar halbauer   C: roman drahosz   P: embers comsulting gmbh

A: embers comsulting gmbh   M: d.halbauer@embers.at

www.sapien.com.br
D: santana dardot, gustavo timponi   C: sapien team
A: sapien   M: santana@sapien.com.br

www.hybride.com
D: jean-francois lemay   C: pascal rousse   P: bungastudio
A: kawabunga   M: sylvie@hybride.com

www.loftlinx.at
D: dietmar halbauer   C: roman drahosz   P: embers comsulting gmbh
A: embers comsulting gmbh   M: d.halbauer@embers.at

www.massimo.es
D: massimo céspedes   C: massimo céspedes   P: massimo céspedes
A: evolulab   M: massimo@evolulab.com

www.thaiwebbiz.com
D: nattanan vepulananda   C: nattanan vepulananda   P: athiwath roongmak
A: thaiwebbiz.com   M: www.thaiwebbiz.com

www.dworkz.com
D: stanislav udotov   C: michael chernobrod   P: vadim dostman
A: d.workz interactive   M: info@dworkz.com

www.saltedherring.com
D: pepijn zuijderwijk
A: saltedherring   M: pep@saltedherring.com

www.botanicadeljibaro.com
D: la mano fria   C: gamebombing   P: beta bodega coalition
A: botanica del jibaro   M: info@betabodega.com

www.lafano.it
D: lafano art direction and technical department   P: lafano s.r.l.
M: d.covre@lafano.it

www.filippasmedhagensund.com
D: hugo ahlberg   C: eduard prats molner   P: mocoro
A: mocoro   M: info@mocoro.com

www.hmtmx.com
D: chi chau lam   C: chi chau lam   P: chi chau lam
A: cO6studio   M: info@cO6studio.com

www.tomter.net
D: sennep
M: jorn@tomter.net

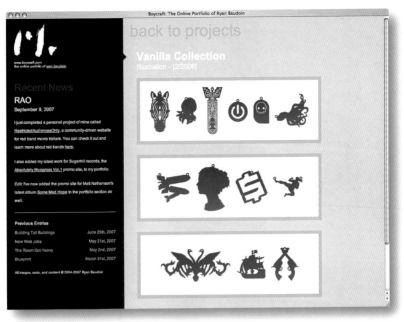

www.boycraft.com
D: ryan baudoin   C: ryan baudoin   P: ryan baudoin
A: ryan baudoin   M: ryan@boycraft.com

www.eatmydear.com
D: markus hornof, patrick sturm   C: marian plösch
A: eat my dear - motion * design * direction   M: info@eatmydear.com

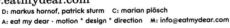

www.macacolandia.com.br
D: mauricio campos zuardi   C: mauricio campos zuardi   P: mauricio campos zuardi
A: macacolândia - simion ddbz estudio de arte   M: simios@macacolandia.com.br

www.benga.li
D: cedric muller   C: cedric muller   P: cedric muller
A: b-tween   M: muller@b-tween.com

www.bertb.net
D: bert bräutigam   C: zoë leblanche   P: brunó bernard
A: farbe   M: hallo@farbe-form.net

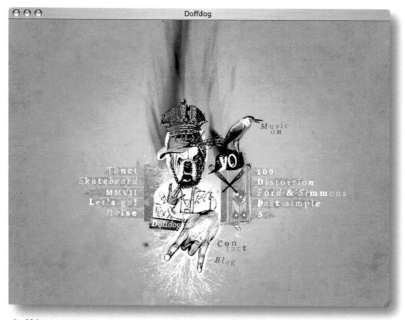

www.doffdog.com
D: alexey potapov
M: doffdog@gmail.com

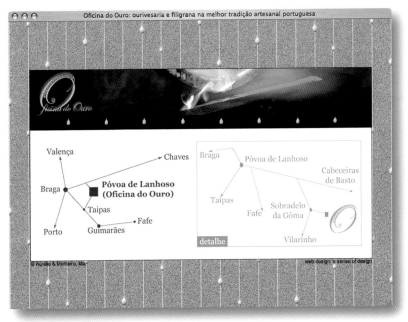

www.oficinadoouro.com
D: roberto gorjão   C: roberto gorjão
M: roberto@castelosnoar.com

www.diecidecimi.tv
D: matteo rostagno   C: riccardo campioni   P: matteo rostagno
A: out of media   M: diecidecimi@diecidecimi.tv

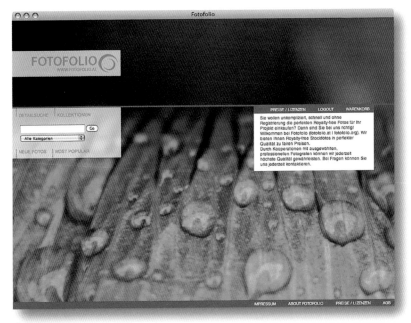

www.fotofolio.at
D: david kitzmüller   C: sigurd buchberger
M: info@fotofolio.at

www.poupine.com.tw

D: alice wu   C: alice wu   P: alice wu

A: poupine   M: dreamily5@gmail.com

www.chiyodaworx.com

D: deivis tavares, lara teang   C: deivis tavares   P: deivis tavares, lara teang

A: chiyodaworx   M: chiyodaworx@chiyodaworx.com

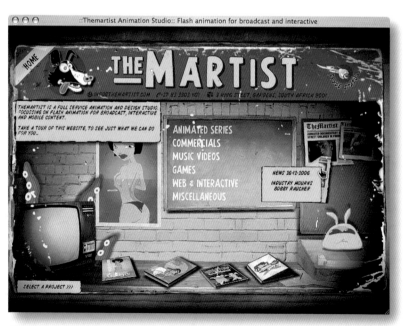

www.themartist.com

D: martin fisher

A: themartist animation studio   M: info@themartist.com

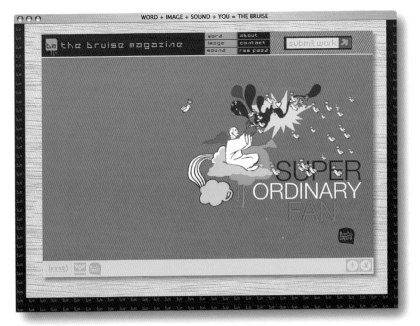

www.thebruise.com
D: mark shepherd   C: mark shepherd   P: mark shepherd
A: brutalgift   M: mark@thebruise.com

www.danielsytsma.nl
D: daniël sytsma   C: simon hattinga verschure
M: email@danielsytsma.nl

www.gaiadepaoli.co.uk
D: gaia de paoli   C: gaia de paoli
A: gaia de paoli   M: gaia@gaiadepaoli.co.uk

www.studiofmmilano.it

D: studio fm milano   C: parkmedia   P: studio fm milano
A: studio fm milano   M: info@studiofmmilano.it

www.garrettworld.co.uk

D: scott garrett   C: graham bates
A: scott garrett   M: scott@garrettworld.co.uk

www.storyvilleonline.com

D: michelangelo petralito, iolanda rotiroti   C: giovanni antico
A: petralito rotiroti associati   M: info@petralitorotirotiassociati.com

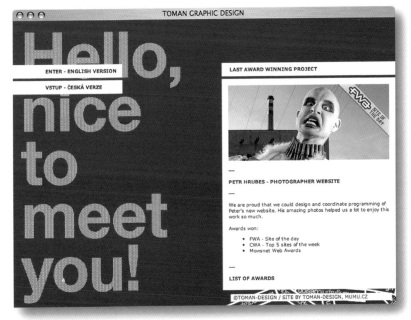

www.toman-design.com

D: david brezina, jiri toman, brano matis   C: roman erlebach   P: jiri toman
A: toman graphic design   M: info@toman-design.com

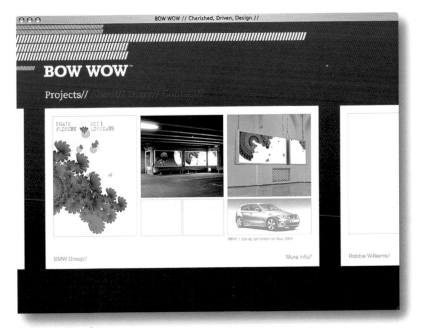

www.bowwowlondon.com

D: bow wow international, sennep   C: sennep   P: bow wow international
A: bow wow international   M: woof@bowwowlondon.com

www.skribbs.com

D: aman singh   C: aman singh   P: aman singh
A: skribbs   M: aman@skribbs.com

www.boxx3g.com
D: enis koch   C: enis koch   P: enis koch
A: boxx3g   M: ignite@boxx3g.com

www.atutiplen.es
D: jerico santander   C: ricardo echegaray   P: carlos yuste
A: taller de ideas atutiplén s.l.   M: carlos@atutiplen.es

www.cofradiadelbuenjesus.org
D: anna maria lopez lopez   C: anna maria lopez lopez   P: anna maria lopez lopez
A: anna-om-line.com   M: hello@anna-om-line.com

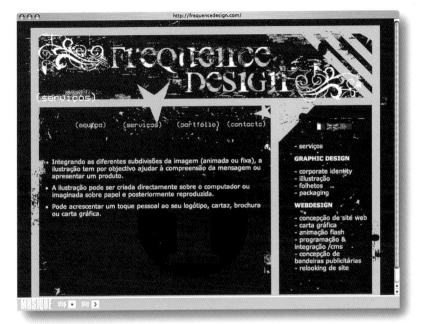

www.frequencedesign.ch
D: rosalia sousa   C: rosalia sousa, nils chatton   P: rosalia
M: info@frequencedesign.com

wefail.com
D: visionworks music
M: info@visionworksmusic.com

www.pixelworx.com.sg
D: francis allan v. andalis   C: francis allan v. andalis   P: james paul pilande
A: pixelworx.com.sg   M: info@pixelworx.com.sg

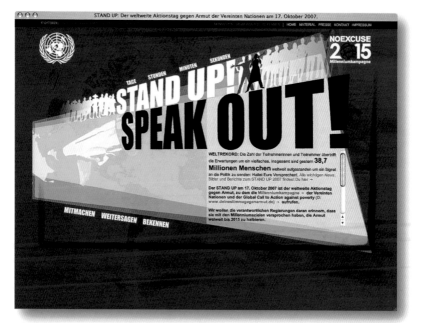

www.stelldichgegenarmut.de
D: schütz, becker   C: spreadlab.com   P: sebastian majewski
A: young   M: redaktion@un-kampagne.de

www.experimentoloizaga.com
D: teofilo riadigos   C: teofilo riadigos   P: teofilo riadigos
A: experimento loizaga   M: info@teofiloriadigos.com

www.edisseny.com
D: emilio garcia vaz   C: emilio garcia vaz
A: edisseny.com   M: emilio@edisseny.com

www.dadan.net
D: ala dadan
M: adi@dadan.net

www.fezuone.com
D: felipe zuleta   C: felipe zuleta   P: felipe zuleta
A: fezuone   M: felipe@fezuone.com

www.svizra.com
D: maurus fraser   C: maurus fraser   P: maurus fraser
A: svizra   M: maurus@svizra.com

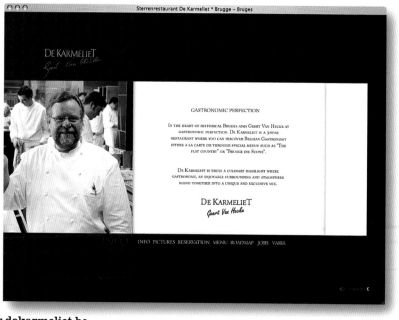

www.dekarmeliet.be
D: frederik vanderfaeillie   C: gaëtan lafaut   P: de karmeliet
A: chilli design   M: www.chilli.be

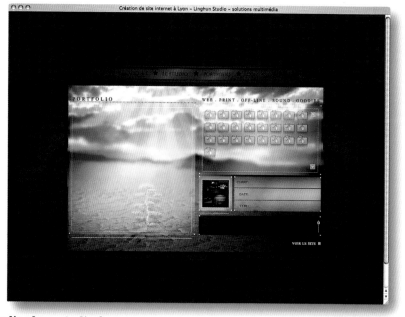

www.linghun-studio.fr
D: sébastien charvolin   C: erik hostein   P: e.hostein, s.charvolin
A: linghün studio   M: contact@linghun-studio.fr

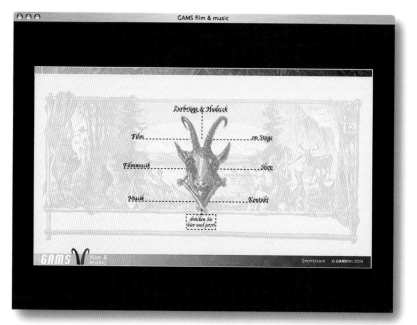

www.gams.cc
D: thomas treu   C: thomas treu
M: ttreu@gmx.net

www.intraligi.com
D: philippe intraligi   C: philippe intraligi   P: philippe intraligi
A: intraligi.com   M: intraligi@gmx.de

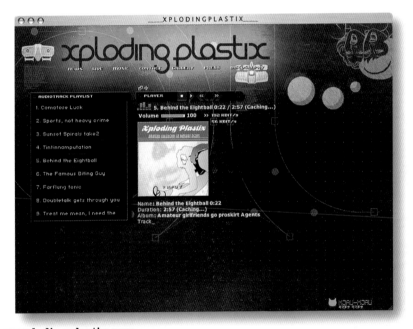

www.xplodingplastix.com
D: mjau-mjau.com
M: mjau@mjau-mjau.com

www.slingshot.co.uk/land
D: mat burhouse   C: mat burhouse, stu harper
A: slingshot   M: hello@slingshot.co.uk

www.huevisualab.com
D: joey khor C: lim seng kai, fizah rahim, mk wong P: rozell ng
A: hue visualab sdn bhd M: info@huevisualab.com

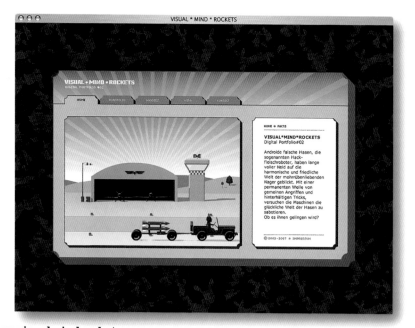

www.visualmindrockets.com
D: daniel woessner C: daniel woessner P: daniel woessner
A: visual*mind*rockets M: woessner@visualmindrockets.com

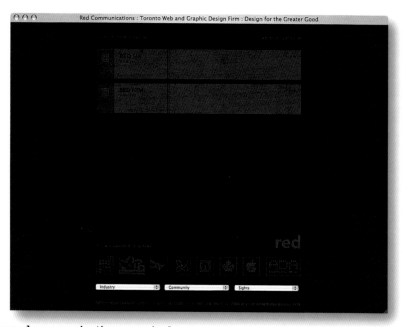

www.redcommunications.com/red_mx
D: paul edward fleming C: paul edward fleming P: curtis achilles
A: red communications M: contact@redcommunications.com

www.3tel.es
D: alfonso corrales   C: enrique valentin morganizo   P: optimo 3tel
A: grapha intuitive   M: www.grapha.net

www.fgs.hu
D: oláh máté   C: gloviczki gábor   P: oláh máté @ fgs
A: fontos graphic design   M: info@fgs.hu

www.wildmarie.de
D: désirée rose   C: marcel ströter
A: desiree-rose.de   M: mail@desiree-rose.de

www.rexbox.co.uk

D: rex crowle

A: rexbox   M: rex@rexbox.co.uk

buded.com

D: igotz ziarreta   C: wordpress

A: deabruk.com   M: igotzu@gmail.com

www.mariolalich.com

D: david skokna   P: mario lalich

A: huge   M: mario@mariolalich.com

www.nussbrennerei.com
D: carsten tischer   C: jens richter
A: tischer grafikbüro+formschön werbeagenturen   M: kontakt@formschoen-agenturen.de

www.packofsix.com
D: jeremy jones   C: jeremy jones   P: jeremy jones
A: jeremy jones   M: jeremy@acheekyhalf.co.uk

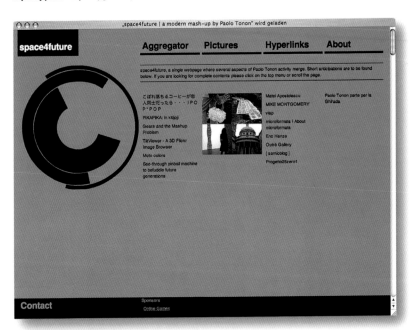

www.space4future.com
D: paolo tonon   C: paolo tonon
M: paolotonon@gmail.com

www.wesc.com/letsgetphysical
D: asbra
A: cocky   M: web@wesc.com

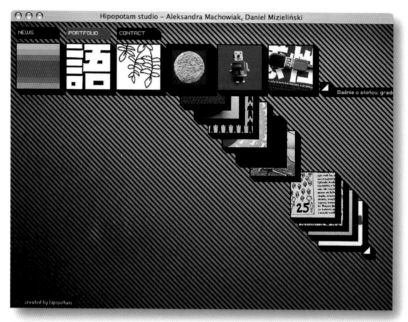

www.hipopotamstudio.pl
D: aleksandra machowiak, daniel mizieliński
A: hipopotam studio   M: kawainka@hipopotamstudio.pl

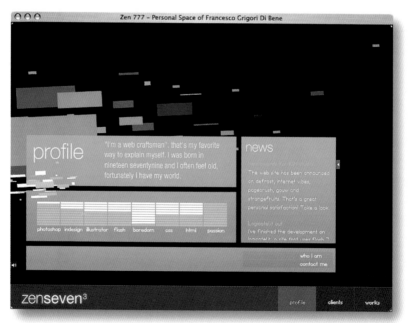

www.zen777.com
D: francesco grigori di bene   C: francesco grigori di bene
A: zen seven 3   M: skiele@gmail.com

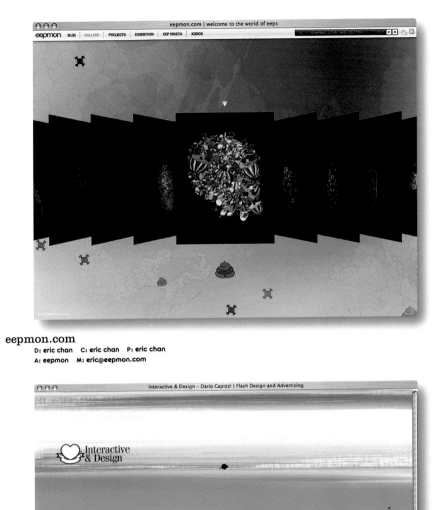

eepmon.com
D: eric chan   C: eric chan   P: eric chan
A: eepmon   M: eric@eepmon.com

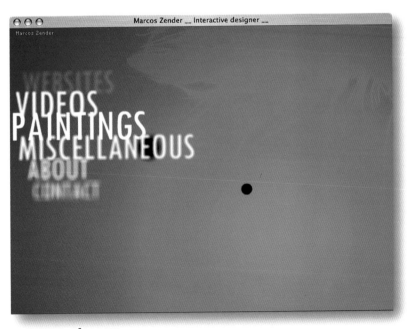

www.interactiveanddesign.com
D: dario capizzi   C: dario capizzi   P: dario capizzi
A: interactive   M: info@interactiveanddesign.com

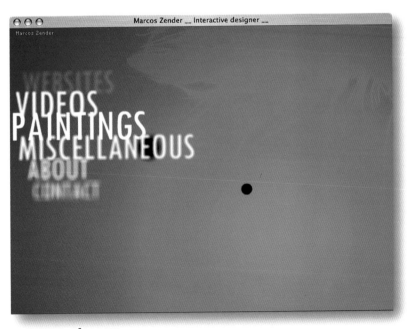

www.marcoszender.com
D: marcos zender   C: marcos zender
M: studio@marcoszender.com

www.claudiadangelo.com
D: enza morello   C: simona galletto   P: enza morello
A: st.francis design.communication   M: enza.morello@stfrancis.it

www.sazacat.net
D: silvia bartoli, davide melis   C: davide melis
M: sazacat@gmail.com

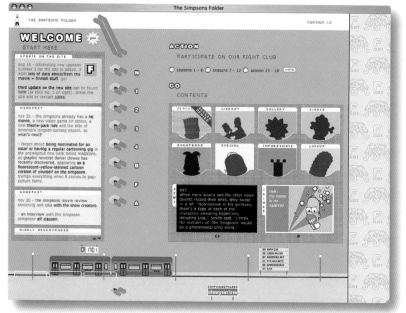

www.simpsonsfolder.com
D: jukka keskiaho
M: jukka.keskiaho@pp.inet.fi

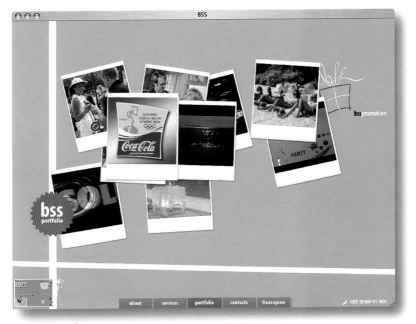

www.bsspromotion.com
D: rizn
A: bss promotion ltd.　M: s.vassilev@bsspromotion.com

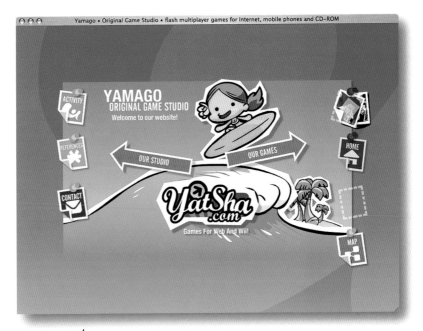

www.yamago.net
D: yamago　C: yamago　P: yamago
A: yamago　M: yamago@yamago.net

www.brandbud.com
D: eddie, allace, kean yew, wei tiong, roland　C: wei tiong, kean yew　P: the bud team
A: bud　M: roland@brandbud.com

www.roottree.ro
D: liviu ceacar C: alin sfetcu
M: contact@roottree.ro

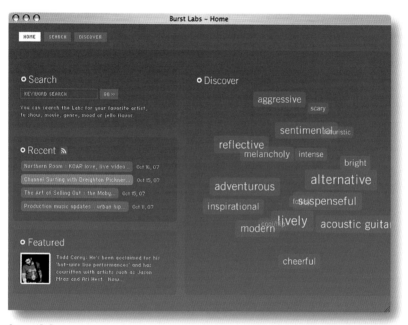

www.burstlabs.com
D: jd hooge, gridplane C: david knape, bumpslide P: jd hooge
A: gridplane M: jd@gridplane.com

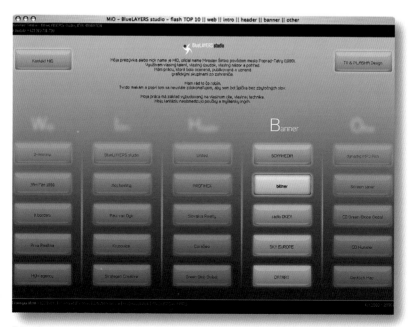

www.bluelayers.com
D: mio miroslav simko C: mio miroslav simko P: mio miroslav simko
A: mio miroslav simko M: web@bluelayers.com

www.loseyourmind.eu

D: tom hulan   C: philipp kyeck, joachim kerkhoff   P: tom hulan
A: blackjune™   M: info@blackjune.com

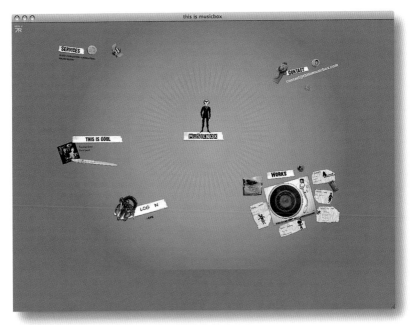

www.thisismusicbox.com

D: teofilo riadigos   C: teofilo riadigos   P: teofilo riadigos
A: music box   M: info@teofiloriadigos.com

www.bucicart.eu

D: christian bucic
M: christian.bucic@bucicart.eu

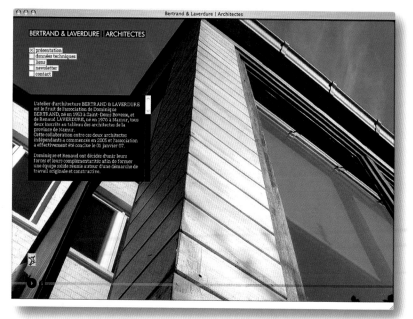

www.bertrand-laverdure.be
D: fx. marciat   C: fx. marciat   P: fx. marciat
A: xy area   M: xy@xyarea.be

www.hirmes.com
D: david hirmes
M: contact@hirmes.com

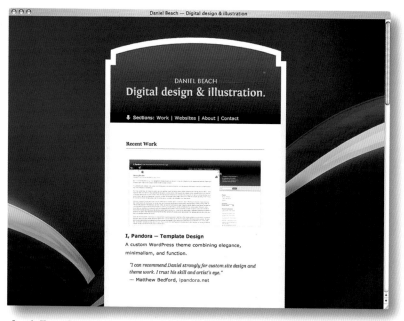

www.danielbeach.com
D: daniel beach
M: email@danielbeach.com

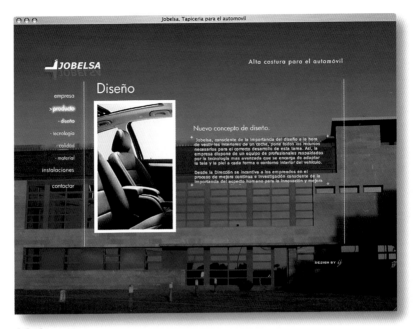

www.jobelsa.com

D: iskiam jara   C: iskiam jara   P: jobelsa
A: iskiam jara estudio de diseño   M: iskiam@iskiamjara.com

www.isar.com.au

D: peter howie   C: lee borowiak   P: peter howie, mark stewart
A: rare identity   M: info@rareid.com.au

www.famewhore.com

D: francis chan   C: francis chan   P: francis chan
A: famewhore   M: ilovefamewhore@gmail.com

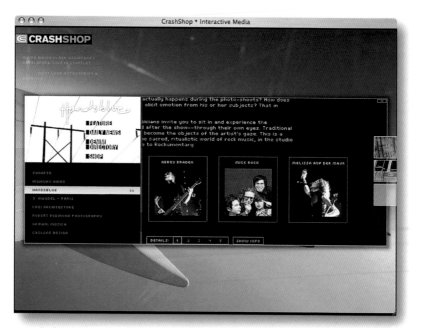

www.crashshop.com

D: michael redmond, jon cook, scott thiessen   C: scott thiessen, michael redmond
A: crashshop   M: info@crashshop.com

www.hidetsugu-m.com

D: hidetsugu murakani
M: info@hidetsugu.com

www.a-mazine.com

D: hristo spasunin   P: hristo spasunin
A: web studio route 75   M: info@route75.com

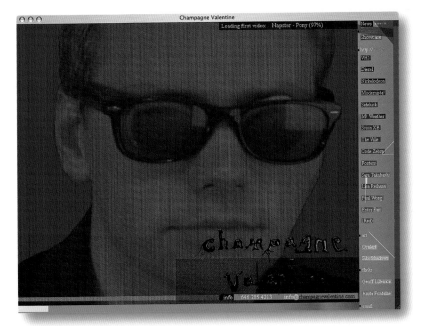

www.champagnevalentine.com
D: geoff lillemon, anita fontaine   C: alex chen, nicholas hillier   P: dexter randazzo
A: champagne valentine   M: info@champagnevalentine.com

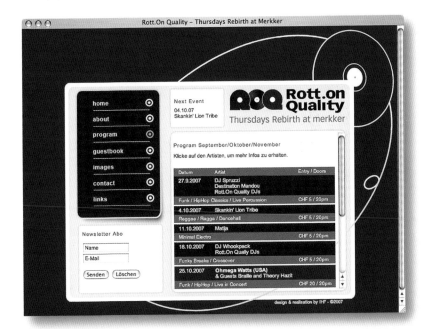

www.rottonquality.ch
D: claude luethi, pascal imhof, yves luethi   C: yves luethi   P: yves luethi
M: ihf@rottonquality.ch

en.heureka.pl
D: www.sullivan.pl, www.heureka.pl   C: www.sullivan.pl   P: www.sullivan.pl
A: heureka (advertising agency)   M: info@heureka.pl

www.glitchanimation.com

D: francis allan v. andalis   C: francis allan v. andalis   P: james paul pilande
A: pixelworx pte. ltd.   M: info@pixelworx.com.sg

www.openfieldcreative.com

D: josh barnes, brandon blangger, brian keenan
A: openfield creative   M: opendialogue@openfieldcreative.com

www.observatoryfilms.com

D: will weyer, todd anderson   C: will weyer, jeff askew   P: matt daly
A: wiretree wiretree.com   M: wiretree.com

www.liquified.com
D: carlos todero   C: gabriel giacomini
A: todero design studio   M: liquified@comcast.net

www.grandlargeinc.com
D: philippe giuntini   P: steven horton
A: grand large inc   M: steven@grandlargeinc.com

www.vgarchitect.it
D: stefania boiano   C: invisiblestudio   P: vg architect
A: invisiblestudio   M: www.invisiblestudio.it

265

www.ercentras.com
    D: gaumina
    M: goda@gaumina.ie

www.tytz.com
    D: bülent sik   C: emre ozyurek   P: burak gunsev
    A: wanda digital   M: www.wandadigital.com

www.bionic-systems.com
    D: doris fürst, malte haust   C: sven elllingen   P: bionic systems
    A: bionic systems   M: info@bionic-systems.com

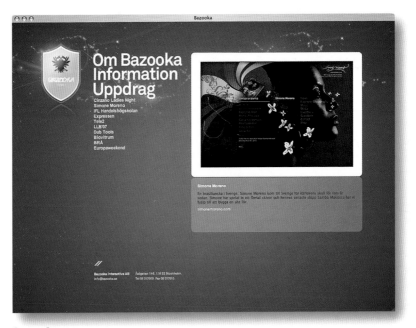

www.bazooka.se
D: andreas pihlström   C: tomas larsson   P: bo valpeters
A: bazooka ab   M: bo@bazooka.se

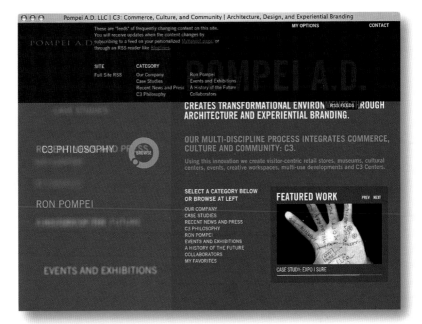

www.pompeiad.com
D: pompei a.d.   C: fl2   P: ron pompei
A: pompei a.d.   M: jnewman@pompeiad.com

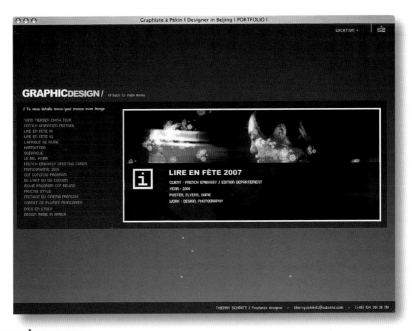

www.subsens.com
D: thierry alexandre schmitt   C: thierry alexandre schmitt   P: thierry alexandre schmitt
A: subsens I design   M: thierry.schmitt@subsens.com

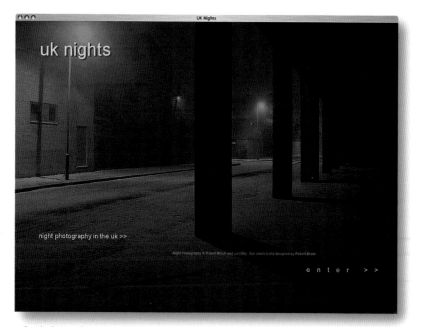

www.uknights.photolucid.com
D: robert brook   C: robert brook
A: robert brook pictures   M: robert@brookpictures.com

www.passage.sk
D: pavel surovi   C: pavel surovi   P: judit lovisek, pavel surovi
A: communication agency   M: info@communicationagency.com

www.imaste-ips.com
D: a. garcía, d.olmos, a.buixaderas,   C: a. palomino, s. alvarez   P: m. arias
A: imaste-ips   M: imaste@imaste-ips.com

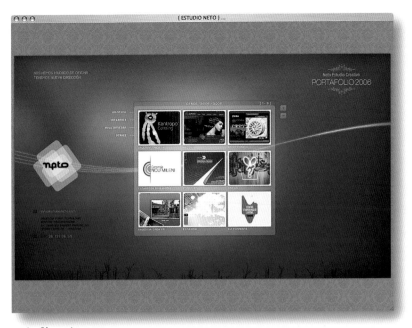

www.estudioneto.com
D: oscar ruiz   C: oscar ruiz   P: jose luis samos baixauli
A: neto estudio creativo   M: info@estudioneto.com

www.bangkok2.com
D: thanawat c. ekalak v. nattavut l.   C: sasis s. chon k.   P: sulichai s. vichai t.
A: bangkoktwo   M: info@bangkok2.com

www.napszel.hu
D: nemeth csaba elek   C: nagy csaba   P: németh csaba elek
A: nap, szél és csillagok bookdesigner ltd.   M: info@napszel.hu

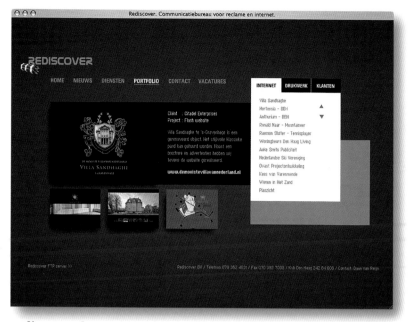

www.rediscover.nl

D: daan van reijn   C: daan van reijn
A: rediscover.nl   M: info@rediscover.nl

www.atds.ch

D: cedric muller   C: cedric muller   P: eric trezza
A: b-tween   M: muller@b-tween.com

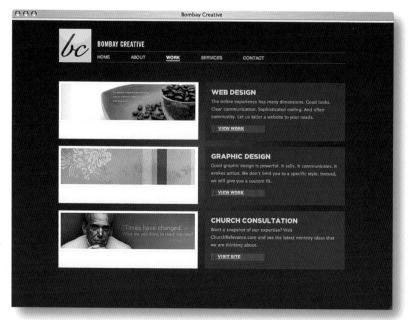

bombaycreative.com

D: evie shaffer   C: evie shaffer
A: bombay creative   M: info@bombaycreative.com

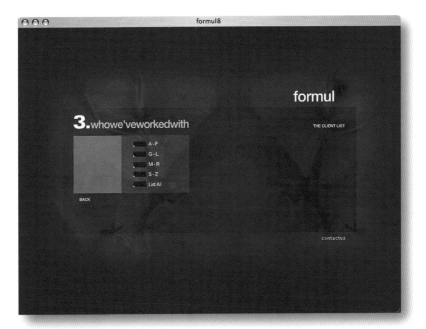

www.formul8.com

D: sam wong   C: mohd jaffry   P: fiona bartholomeusz
A: formul8 private limited   M: fiona@formul8.com

STAY TUNED

www.mocoro.com

D: hugo ahlberg   C: eduard prats molner   P: mocoro
A: mocoro   M: info@mocoro.com

www.iamsia.com

D: sia ashegh   C: emanuel adams   P: sia ashegh
M: sia.ashegh@gmail.com

www.flow4.com

D: florian alcantara   C: florian alcantara   P: florian alcantara
A: flow4 gmbh & co. kg   M: f.alcantara@flow4.com

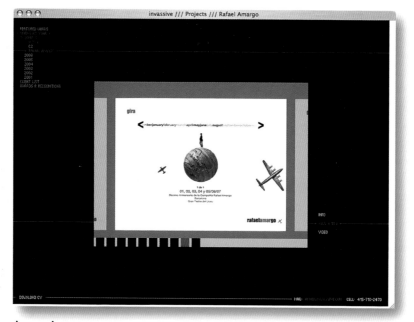

www.invassive.com

D: iñigo orduña   C: omar rodriguez   P: omar rodriguez
A: invassive   M: omar@invassive.com

www.drhapgill.com

D: miroslav koljanin   C: miroslav koljanin   P: miroslav koljanin
A: www.drawingart.org   M: info@drhapgill.com

www.crestklcc.com
D: syazwin hayati C: surayati P: ridzwan
A: acdra web design M: www.crestklcc.com/contact.html

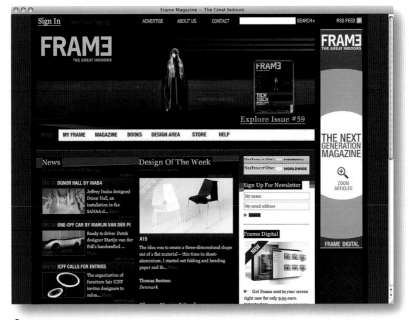

www.framemag.com
D: bornO5 C: bornO5 P: bornO5
A: frame publishers M: rogier@bornO5.nl

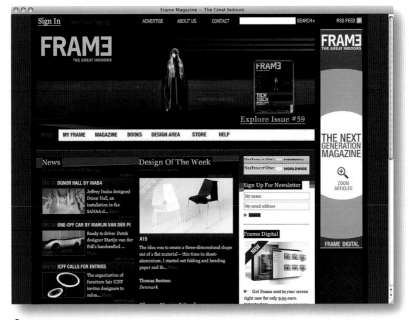

www.evoland.es
D: javier alvear ruiz-rivas
M: info@evoland.es

www.moonpalace.fr

D: alexandre soubrier   C: alexandre soubrier   P: alexandre soubrier

M: alex@moonpalace.fr

www.eskalation.com

D: martin van den hoogen

A: eskalation I design, illustration, art direction   M: info@eskalation.com

www.evokelabs.com

D: adrian pikios   C: adrian pikios

A: evoke labs   M: adrian@evokelabs.com

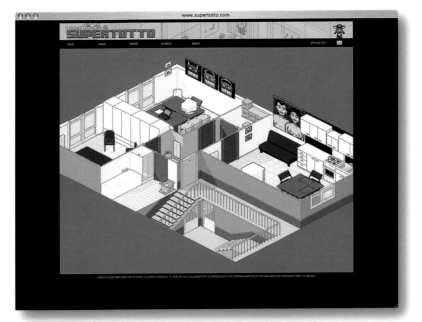

www.supertotto.com
D: totto renna
A: supertotto   M: info@supertotto.com

www.c505.com
D: yoshi sodeoka
M: y@c505.com

www.ccbng.com
D: cocobongo artworks   C: cocobongo artworks   P: cocobongo artworks
A: cocobongo artworks   M: cocobongo@ccbng.com

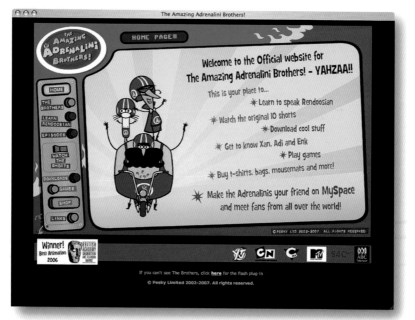

www.waferaudio.com/wafer.html

D: kelly kannisto   C: kelly kannisto   P: paul james
A: wafer audio limited   M: paul.james@waferaudio.com

www.onesize.nl

D: robbert slotman, bart heesink   C: robbert slotman, bart heesink
A: de ruimte ontwerpers   M: info@de-ruimte-ontwerpers.nl

www.foan82.com

D: foan   C: foan   P: foan
A: ruadesign   M: mail@foan82.com

www.neotokio.it
D: rosario valente
A: neotokio! comunicazione visiva   M: info@neotokio.it

www.elitefashion.it
D: giuseppe caruso   C: renato caruso   P: giuseppe caruso
A: lab77 multimedia studio   M: info@lab77.it

www.trautenberk.com
D: jan krátk⬚   C: ladislav brychta   P: jan krátk⬚ at studio cabinet
A: cabinet, www.studiocabinet.com   M: honza@studiocabinet.com

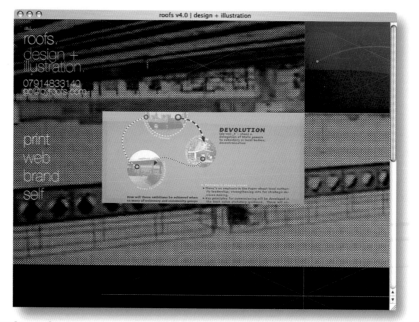

www.byroofs.com

D: agnieszka garofeanu   C: felix turner   P: agnieszka garofeanu
A: roofs | design illustration   M: go@byroofs.com

www.wiiik.com/main.html

D: katia jehel, fredd jehel   C: frédéric benoit   P: katia jehel, fredd jehel
A: wiiik   M: katia@wiiik.com

www.lanzallamas.tv

D: teofilo riadigos, ezequiel black   C: teofilo riadigos   P: m repetto i moiseeff
A: lanzallamas   M: info@teofiloriadigos.com

www.atelierdetour.ch

D: baptiste cochard   C: baptiste cochard   P: baptiste cochard

A: atelier détour   M: info@atelierdetour.ch

www.pilar.it

D: alessandro d'alessandro   C: alessandro d'alessandro   P: alessandro d'alessandro

A: touch creative lab   M: dale@hellomynameis.it

simplesquare.com

D: john furness   C: john furness   P: john furness

A: simple square   M: info@simplesquare.com

www.magwerk.com

D: daniel tveiten, kent løset, perk   C: eirik broen, paulo fierro   P: joakim nilsen

A: blogform digital magazines gmbh   M: joakim.nilsen@blogform.de

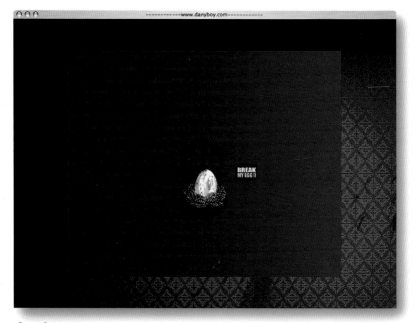

www.danyboy.com

D: dany   C: 16ar   P: dany

A: danyboy   M: dany@semperultimo.com

ladio.ru

D: vladislav troshin   C: alexander antonov

A: ladio   M: vlad@ladio.ru

www.floydph.com
D: gilles abenhaïm **C:** gilles abenhaïm **P:** gilles abenhaïm
A: floyd studio **M:** contact@floydst.com

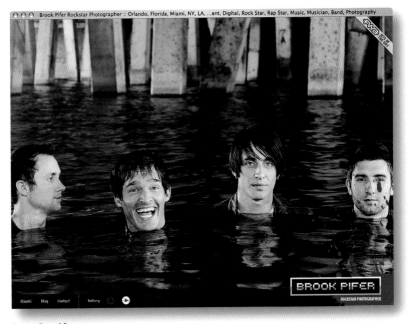

www.brook-pifer.com
D: mat gaver **C:** mat gaver **P:** brook pifer
A: brook pifer - rockstar photographer **M:** studio@brook-pifer.com

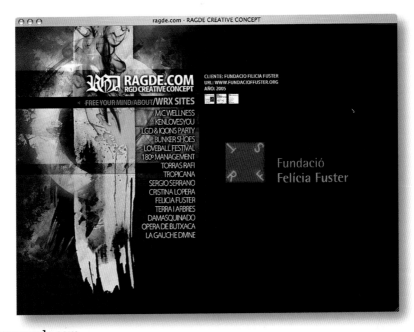

www.ragde.com
D: ragde **C:** ragde **P:** ragde
A: rgd creative concept **M:** www.ragde.com

www.3am-design.com

D: jody poole   C: jody poole   P: adam christl
A: 3am design   M: jody@3am-design.com

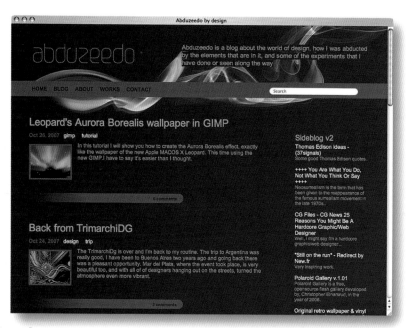

abduzeedo.com

D: fábio sasso   C: fábio sasso
M: fabio.sasso@gmail.com

www.quovadis-simulation.de/src/index.php

D: joerg meister   C: joerg meister
M: www.quovadis-simulation.de

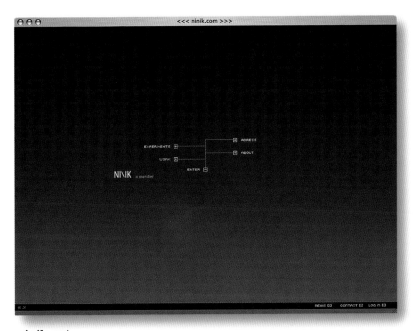

www.ninik.net
D: ninik vogelsang   C: artificialduck studio   P: artificialduck studio, ninik vogelsang
A: ninik   M: info@ninik.com

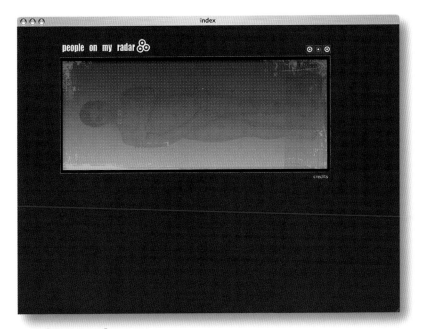

www.peopleonmyradar.com
D: teofilo riadigos, sara huber   C: eric goodwin   P: teofilo riadigos, sara huber
M: info@teofiloriadigos.com

www.domineydesign.com
D: todd dominey   C: todd dominey   P: todd dominey
A: dominey design inc.   M: todd@domineydesign.com

www.organicgrid.com
D: michael mcdonald   C: max liberman
A: organic grid   M: michael@organicgrid.com

www.megcriativos.com
D: diogo ricardo   C: diogo ricardo   P: miguel serôdio
A: meg - produções criativas e intelectuais, lda   M: miguelserodio@megcriativos.com

www.aquakine.be
D: ram broekaert
A: mediamind   M: www.mediamind.be

www.annekabouke.com

D: merijn straathof   C: merijn straathof   P: hanno groen
A: aaaaaaa international group, hongkong, amsterdam   M: info@annekabouke.com

eekanomic.com

D: jean pierre guevremont   C: jean pierre guevremont   P: jean pierre guevremont
M: jp@eekanomic.com

www.storyville.com

D: will weyer   C: jeff askew, robb bennett, will weyer, ryan taylor
A: wiretree   M: wiretree.com

www.bureaudetabas.com

D: cedric malo C: km817 P: tabas
A: tabas M: cedric@tabas.fr

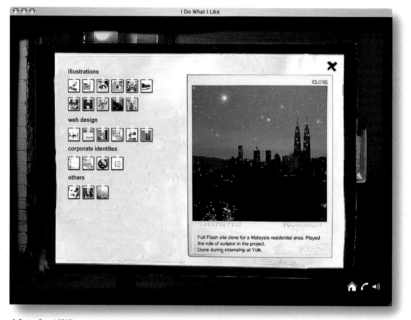

www.idowhatilike.com

D: lim yian phing C: lim yian phing P: lim yian phing
A: personal portfolio site M: yplim@idowhatilike.com

www.themixhead.com

D: ulyana kalashnikova
M: mixheadinfo@gmail.com

www.fisticuffdesign.com
D: rene vazquez   C: bryan miller   P: bryan miller, rene vazquez
A: fisticuff design co.   M: rene@fisticuffdesign.com

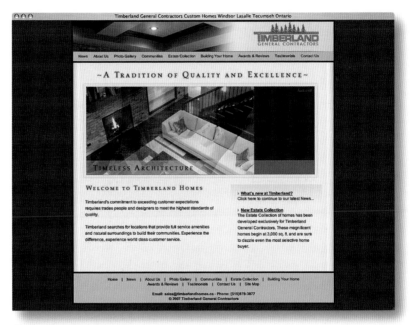

www.timberlandhomes.ca
D: heike delmore   C: wired solutions   P: heike delmore
A: jack in the web   M: info@jackintheweb.ca

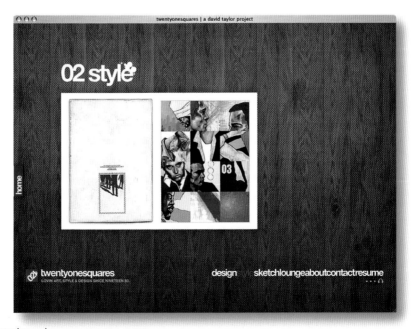

www.twentyonesquares.com
D: david taylor
A: twentyonesquares   M: info@21squares.com

www.gertrudis.com

D: txarly brown   C: manel freire   P: manel freire
A: victobit informática   M: info@gertrudis.com

www.julianabraz.com.br

D: peterson silva   C: eduardo hayashi, peterson silva   P: gilberto freitas
A: aliens design   M: gilberto@aliensdesign.com.br

www.takeone.es

D: lourdes molina, daniel vico, manu martin   C: marcos q-interactiva   P: takeone dsgn
A: takeone dsgn   M: tk1@takeone.es

www.testemale-photos.com

D: jero-m C: jero-m, antoine malpel, thierry bugeat
A: infoborn M: jerome@infoborn.com

www.lbctop20.com

D: elastic people
M: info@lbctop20.com

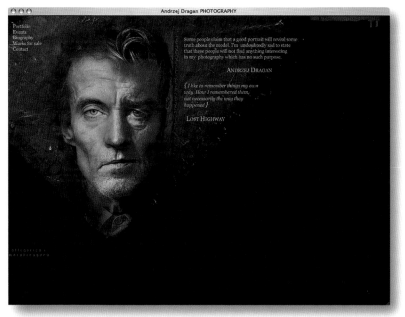

andrzejdragan.com

D: andrzej dragan C: michal barteczko P: andrzej dragan
A: andrzej dragan M: mail@andrzejdragan.com

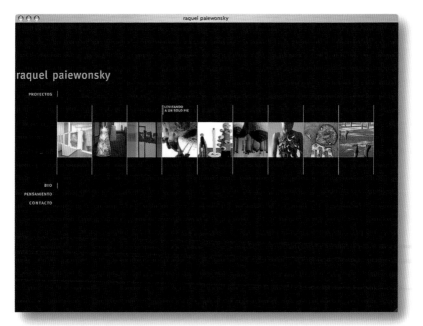

www.raquelpaiewonsky.com
D: irina miolan   C: jose garcia   P: raquel paiewonsky
A: equipo3 web design   M: el_flashco@yahoo.com

www.davidhuhnband.de
D: peter ulrich   C: peter ulrich   P: peterulrich.net
A: peterulrich.net   M: peter@peterulrich.net

www.kryszpin.net
D: andrzej kryszpiniuk
A: kryszpin   M: kryszpin@kryszpin.net

www.blogsolid.com

D: imar krige

M: imar@abovethemedia.com

www.tado.co.uk

D: mike doney, katie tang

A: tado   M: mikeandkatie@tado.co.uk

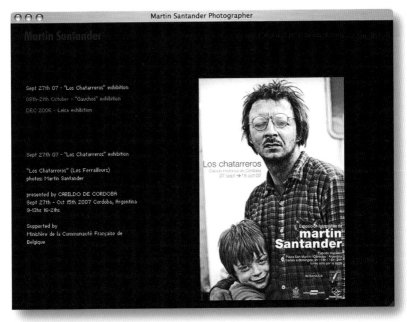

www.martinsantander.com

D: arnaud beelen   C: alexandre lamberty   P: martin santander

A: martin santander   M: martin@martinsantander.com

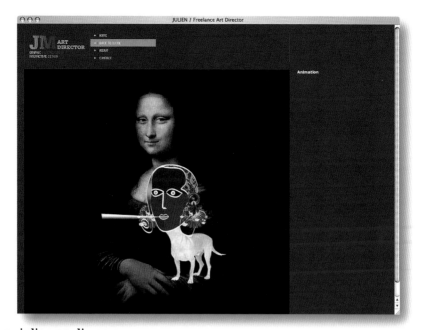

www.julienmoulin.com
D: julien moulin
A: julien moulin   M: julien.design@gmail.com

www.iseedeadpixels.nl
D: sander rietdijk   C: arjen gosman   P: sander rietdijk
A: i see dead pixels   M: info@iseedeadpixels.nl

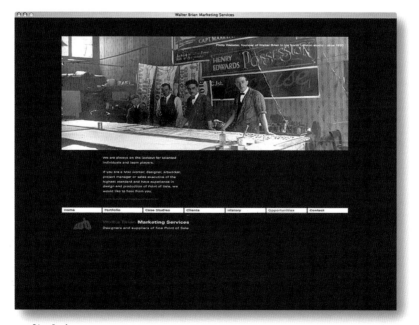

www.walterbrian.com
D: shariff moossun, martin webster   C: shariff moossun
A: tamarin design limited   M: studio@tamarin.co.uk

www.vicho4d.com
D: vinicio lopez   C: vinicio lopez   P: vinicio lopez
A: magikal urbania   M: vicho4d@yahoo.com

www.qwst.com
D: bartek golebiowski, adam nieszporek   C: jacek zakowicz, wojecich rymaszewski
A: click5   M: info@click5.pl

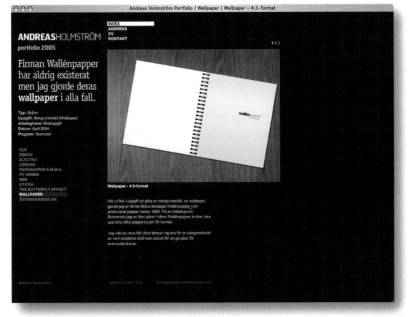

www.andreasholmstrom.com
D: andreas holmström   C: andreas holmström   P: andreas holmström
A: andreas holmström produktion   M: andreas@andreasholmstrom.com

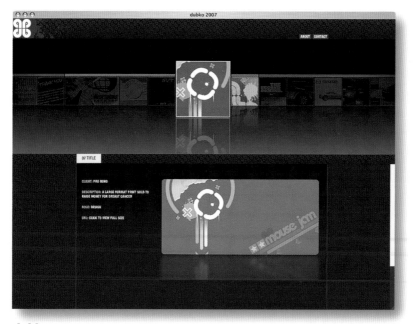

www.dubko.com

D: james kowalski   C: james kowalski
A: dubko   M: james@dubko.com

www.cosmit.it

D: stefano balossi, cosmit spa   C: gruppo 36   P: cosmit spa
A: cosmit spa   M: info@cosmit.it

www.velvetgoldmine.eu

D: giuseppe caruso   C: renato caruso   P: giuseppe caruso
A: lab77 multimedia studio   M: info@lab77.it

www.hellocolor.com

D: pawel nolbert   C: pawel nolbert   P: pawel nolbert
A: hellocolor   M: color@hellocolor.com

www.mosk.pl

D: mciej mizer   C: jakub slaby   P: maciej mizer
M: mosk@mosk.pl

www.dougshimizu.com

D: john godfrey   C: casey britt   P: doug shimizu
A: doug shimizu photography   M: info@dougshimizu.com

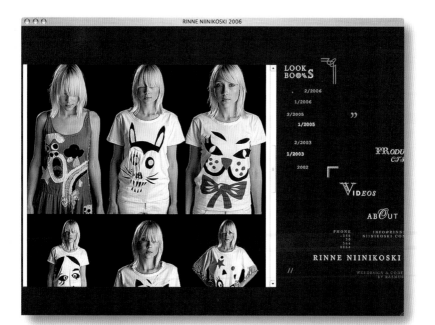

www.rinneniinikoski.com

D: rasmus snabb   C: rasmus snabb   P: piia rinne, noora niinikoski

A: rinne niinikoski   M: info@rinneniinikoski.com

www.srown.com

D: alex djordjevic   C: alex djordjevic   P: alex djordjevic

A: srown design studio   M: www.srown.com

www.aeform.net

D: alexander radsby   C: alexander radsby   P: alexander radsby

M: alex.radsby@gmail.com

www.ns3d.com

D: nicholas creevy   C: erik hallander   P: nicholas creevy
A: nsthreed   M: nick@ns3d.com

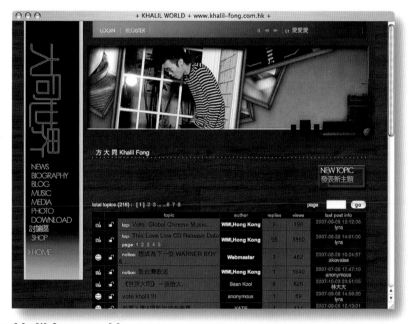

www.khalil-fong.com.hk

D: christotrian tong, miles lam, dee lam   C: christotrian tong, miles lam   P: christotrian tong
A: dash co.   M: info@dash.com.hk

www.bergmann-metallbau.de

D: andreas hilber, christoph rager   C: christoph rager, andreas hilber
A: www.decadeone.com   M: mail@decadeone.com

www.sheeladaley.com
D: gene smirnov   P: tom bergey
A: bergey creative group   M: genes@bcgrouponline.com

www.profission.com
D: tim jarvis   C: rob wilkins   P: alex froom
A: the profission partnership   M: hello@profission.com

www.insignia.pl
D: marcin krawczynski   C: piotr gejgalis, marek brun   P: tomasz michalik
A: insignia interactive agency   M: office@insignia.pl

www.alessiopizzicannella.com
D: www.drinkcreativity.com C: fabio de gregorio P: drink creativity
A: drink creativity M: info@alessiopizzicannella.com

www.fantaskis.com
D: heath taskis C: heath taskis
A: fantaskis design M: heath@fantaskis.com

www.laguarderiateatre.com
D: xevi vilardell bascompte C: xevi vilardell bascompte P: xevi vilardell bascompte
A: xelu.net M: xevi@xelu.net

www.malamujer.es

D: maria malo, miguel fernandez
A: lolita canalla s.l.   M: malamujer@malamujer.es

www.noventaynueve.com/2007

D: carlos ulloa   C: carlos ulloa   P: carlos ulloa
A: carlosulloa.com   M: info@carlosulloa.com

www.exploreibsen.com

D: erlend istad   C: christian westerberg thoresen, a. dirdal   P: oslo public library
A: soulpolice   M: reinertm@deichman.no

www.rgraffiks.com

D: jose miguel serna   M: jms@rgraffiks.com

A: realgraffiks

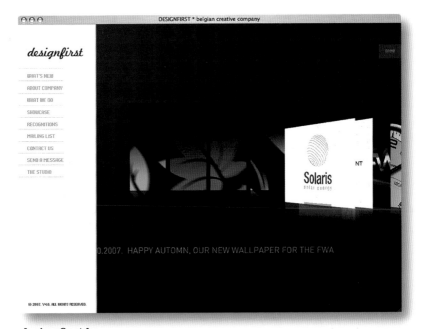

www.designfirst.be

D: olivier piedboeuf   C: team@designfirst

A: designfirst   M: o.piedboeuf@designfirst.be

www.netdesign.cl

D: alvaro parrague   C: alvaro parrague   P: alvaro parrague

A: netdesign   M: alvaro@netdesign.cl

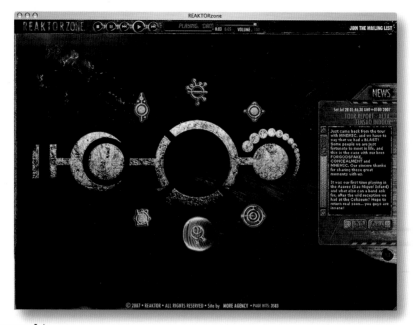

www.reaktorzone.com

D: pedromau   C: pedromau   P: pedromau
A: bad thiseyenz   M: pedromau@hotmail.com

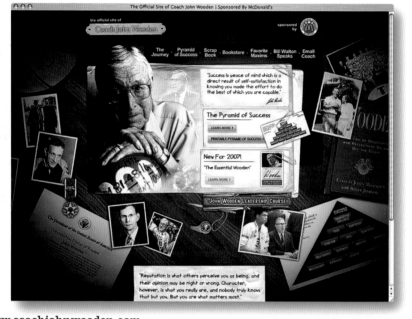

www.coachjohnwooden.com

D: john ryan   C: jason yapp
A: uncommon thinking   M: info@uncommonthinking.com

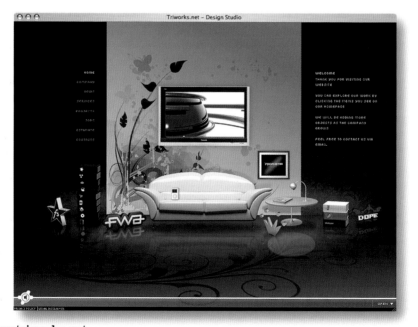

www.triworks.net

D: joao guimaraes   C: joão figueiredo, romulo armas, nuno neves   P: joao guimaraes
A: triworks.net - design studio   M: comercial@triworks.net

www.xentrabs.it
D: nicola scotto di carlo, roberto di tonto   P: xentra business school
A: novantanovepercento I studio   M: studio@novantanovepercento.it

www.cocoe.com
D: cocoe   C: cocoe   P: cocoe
A: the cocoe conspiracy   M: info@cocoe.com

www.ichikoo.com
D: ichikoo, tonic   C: tonic   P: ichikoo
A: ichikoo productions   M: james@ichikoo.com

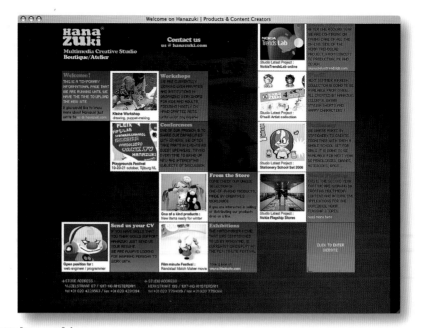

www.hanazuki.com
D: niko stumpo   C: twodotone   P: niko stumpo, hanneke metselaar
A: the hanazuki company   M: h@hanazuki.com

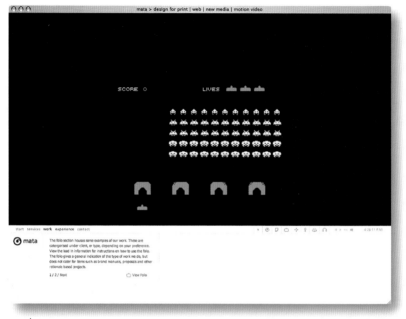

www.mata.co.nz
D: matthew allen   C: matthew allen
A: mata limited   M: mata@mata.co.nz

www.teofiloriadigos.com
D: teofilo riadigos   C: teofilo riadigos   P: teofilo riadigos
A: teofilo riadigos   M: info@teofiloriadigos.com

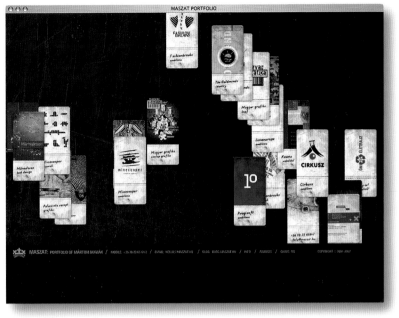

www.maszat.hu
D: márton borzák   C: márton borzák, zoltán fehér
M: hello@maszat.hu

www.emesstyle.com
D: matthew soriano   C: matthew soriano   P: matthew soriano
A: emés   M: matt@emesstyle.com

www.ya3.has.it
D: yakub erogul
A: pilgrim media   M: yakub@pilgrimmedia.com.au

305

www.fabiodeangelis.com

D: giovanni mori   C: giovanni mori
A: katmandudesign   M: info@katmandudesign.it

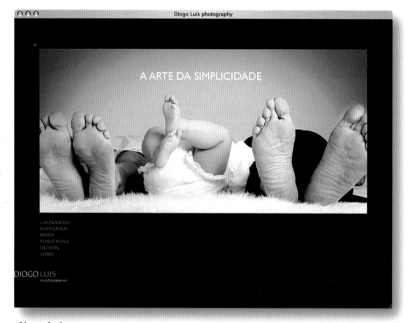

www.diogoluis.com

D: adriano esteves, alexandre gomes   C: alexandre gomes,   P: bürocratik
A: bürocratik   M: info@burocratik.com

www.daddy-design.com

D: pierre elie coursac, peter constantineanu
A: daddy design   M: daddy@daddy-design.com

www.baobabproducciones.com
D: alejandro gonzález   C: alejandro gonzález   P: baobab producciones
A: baobab producciones   M: agonzalez@watchbear.com

www.veljkoonjin.com
D: veljko onjin   C: veljko onjin
M: veljanda@gmail.com

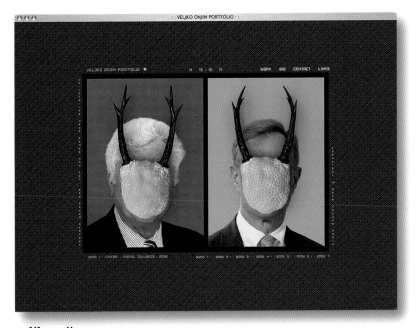

www.sugarfreeink.com
D: alt12O, sugarfreeink   C: alt12O comunicació interactiva   P: alt12O comunicació interactiva
A: alt12O comunicació interactiva   M: contact@alt12O.com

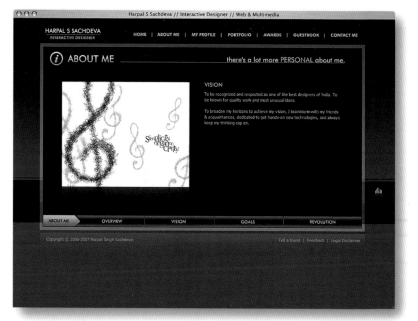

www.harpalsingh.com

D: harpal singh sachdeva   C: harpal singh sachdeva   P: harpal singh sachdeva
A: harpalsingh.com   M: hsingh12@sapient.com

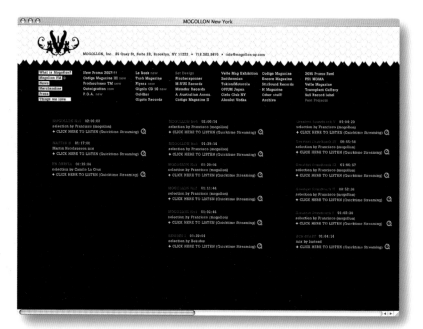

www.mogollon-ny.com

D: francisco lopez   C: francisco lopez   P: francisco lopez
A: mogollon, inc   M: info@mogollon-ny.com

www.vimaxbeauty.com.br

D: peewee   C: peewee   P: peewee
A: peewee.com.br   M: eu@peewee.com.br

www.ericceccarini.com
D: arnaud beelen   C: alexandre lamberty   P: eric ceccarini
A: eric ceccarini   M: ericceccarini@mac.com

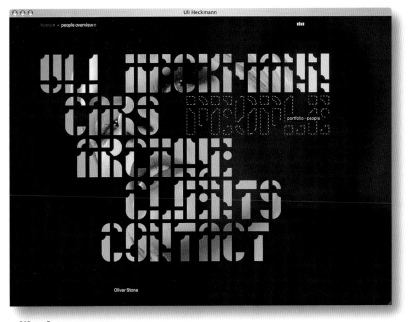

www.uliheckmann.com
D: mikkel due pedersen   C: thomas meyer   P: lars eberle
A: less rain, berlin   M: uli.heckmann@mac.com

www.ultrasonata.com
D: philippe ahmadpanah   C: caroline tissandier
M: philippe@ultrasonata.com

www.rosecglasses.es

D: luis manuel mas orts   C: miguel cartagena, carlos maciá
M: ecologik@gmail.com

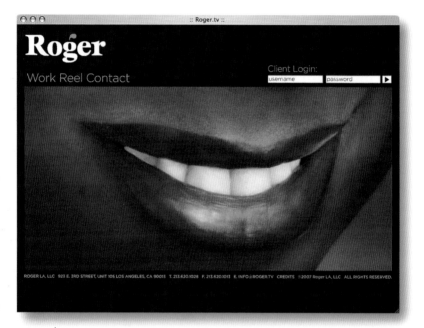

www.roger.tv

D: roger   C: matt ramey   P: sarah cole
A: roger   M: info@roger.tv

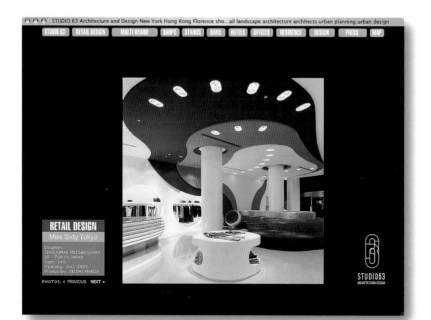

www.studio63.it

D: alessio papi   C: alessio papi   P: alessio papi
A: nextopen multimedia   M: www.nextopen.it

www.djmweb.com

D: dominic marchant   C: patrick frew   P: dominic marchant
A: djm digital solutions ltd   M: info@djmweb.com

www.ksicardo.com

D: kiki sicardo   C: kiki sicardo   P: kiki sicardo
A: k. sicardo   M: altas@ksicardo.com

www.circulocreativo.com.mx

D: miguel salcedo   C: fede puopolo martín bianculli   P: martín lópez eugenio maillefert
A: www.surimimedia.com   M: info@surimimedia.com

www.danielklajmic.com
D: tonho
A: quinta-feira   M: domingo@quinta-feira.org

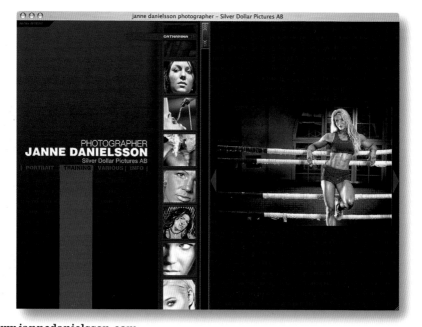

www.jannedanielsson.com
D: mikael österberg   C: mikael österberg   P: mikael österberg
A: webbstudion   M: mikael.osterberg@ekuriren.se

www.blackmintdesign.co.uk
D: matthew paterson
M: mint@blackmintdesign.co.uk

www.soflashe.com

D: piotr kowalczyk   C: skalawwa   P: soflashe
A: soflashe design studio   M: peter@soflashe.com

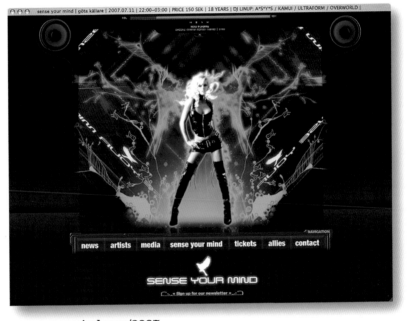

www.senseyourmind.com/2007

D: mikael österberg   C: mikael österberg   P: mikael österberg
A: webbstudion   M: mikael.osterberg@ekuriren.se

philipkonya.com/main.html

D: philip konya   C: philip konya   P: philip konya
A: philip konya   M: info@philipkonya.com

www.a320.dk

D: flemming rasmussen   C: flemming rasmussen   P: flemming rasmussen
A: studio a320   M: flemming@a320.dk

beestudio.pl

D: pawel schedler, piotr korczyński   C: jacek apanasik   P: beestudio
A: beestudio   M: bee@beestudio.pl

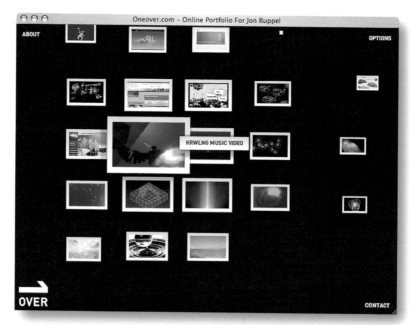

www.oneover.com

D: jon ruppel   C: jon ruppel   P: jon ruppel
A: oneover   M: info@oneover.com

calamityphysics.com

D: matt sundstrom, marisha pessl   C: shea gonyo, brian kadar   P: mark ferdman
A: freedom interactive design   M: mark@freedominteractivedesign.com

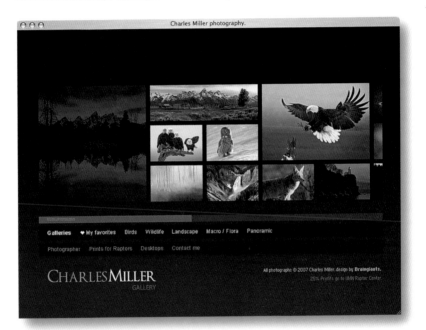

www.braingiants.com/photo

D: charles miller   C: charles miller   P: charles miller
A: braingiants   M: charlie@braingiants.com

www.solarthefilm.com

D: ian wharton, edward shires
A: wharton, shires   M: solar@solarthefilm.com

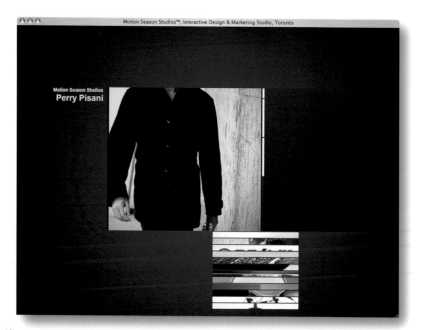

motionseason.com
D: karl pawlowicz   C: michael griffith   P: karl pawlowicz, stéphane bigue
A: motion season studios inc.   M: info@motionseason.com

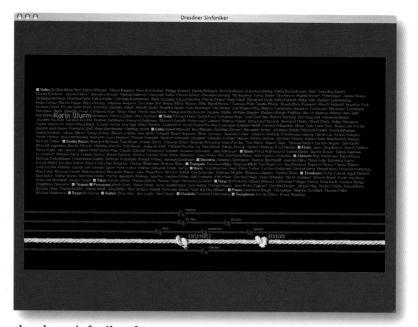

www.dresdner-sinfoniker.de
D: dominik schech   C: dominik schech
A: schech.net   M: kontakt@schech.net

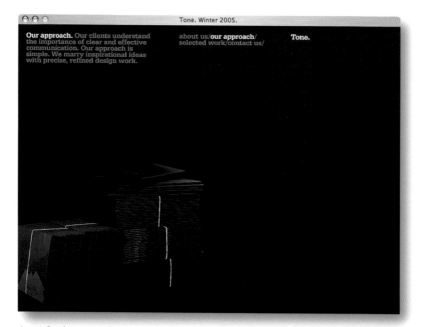

www.tonedesign.co.uk
D: tony phillips   C: tony phillips   P: tony phillips
A: tone design   M: tony@tonedesign.co.uk

www.nastuh.com
D: noe, kreutzer   C: gülensoy, kreuder, hermann, kraft   P: tannenberger, brockmann
A: scholz & volkmer gmbh, wiesbaden   M: www.s-v.de

www.darkforest.tv
D: chandler owen
A: dark forest   M: info@darkforest.tv

www.flyer104.com
D: manuel lópez (fossi)   C: david garcia, jose luis vázquez   P: samuel sánchez
A: flyer104   M: fossi@flyer104.com

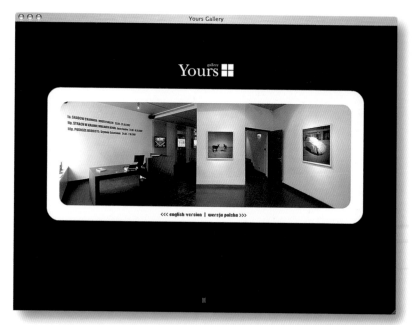

www.yoursgallery.pl
D: marek mielnicki   C: andrzej marchlewski   P: mielnickidesign
A: mielnickidesign   M: info@mielnickidesign.com

www.andreavecchiatophotography.com
D: davide g. aquini
A: whynet.info   M: www.whynet.info

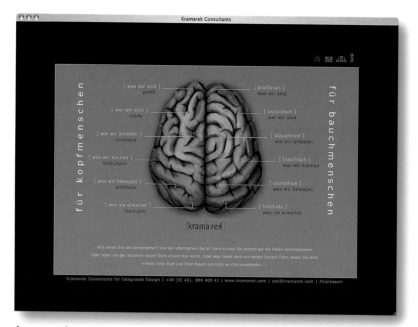

www.kramarek.com
D: johannes kramarek   C: kerstin kramarek   P: kramarek consultants
A: kramarek consultants   M: ask@kramarek.com

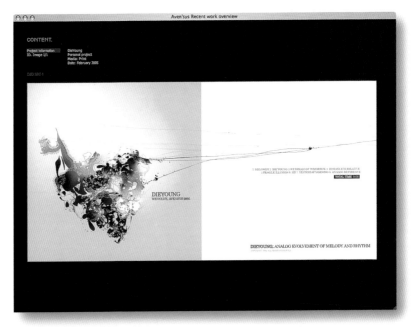

www.avensys.org
D: jort braam   C: jort braam   P: jort braam
A: blör studio   M: jort@avensys.org

www.peteredison.com
D: blanco   C: blanco   P: blanco
A: blanco   M: info@studioblanco.it

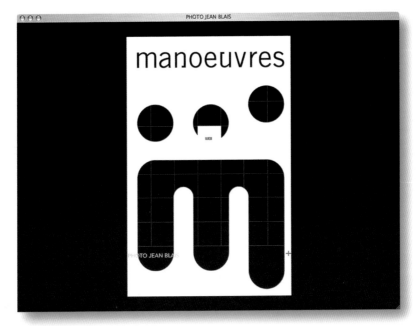

www.jeanblais.com
D: frederic blache   C: frederic blache   P: frederic blache
A: frederic blache design   M: info@fredericblache.com

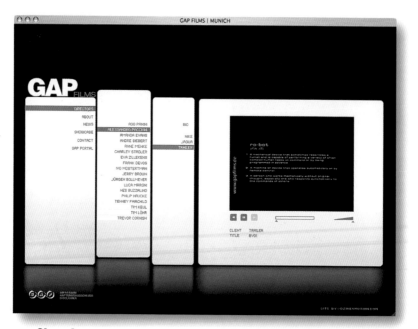

www.gapfilms.de
D: rose pietrovito   C: rose pietrovito   P: rose pietrovito
A: dzinemotion   M: simon@gapfilms.de

www.backstageproductions.es
D: peinados maribel   C: montserrat diaz, enric   P: backstage productions
A: backstage productions   M: blanca@backstageproductions.es

www.primerinc.com
D: lawrence o'toole, lee lilly, brian isserman   C: lee lilly
A: primer   M: info@primerinc.com

www.kelvinzhao.net

D: kelvin zhao   C: kelvin zhao
M: takingovertheworld@gmail.com

www.trioshka.com

D: jon gonzález de amezúa   C: jon gonzález de amezúa   P: productora trioshka
A: amegraf   M: contacto@amegraf.com

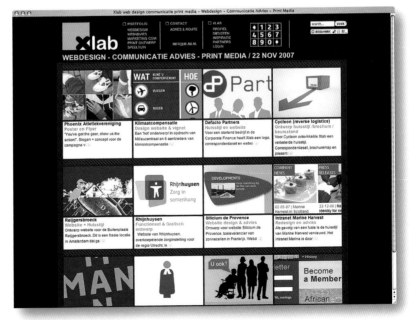

www.xlab.nl

D: iris wilbrink   C: mike bachman   P: roel van cruchten
A: xlab   M: info@xlab.nl

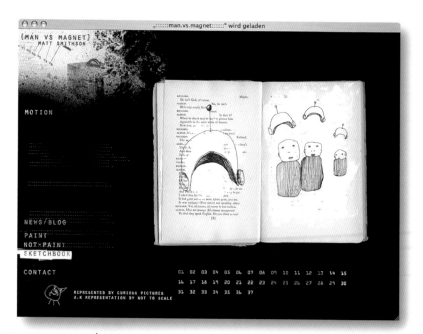

www.manvsmagnet.com
D: matt smithson
A: manvsmagnet   M: www.manvsmagnet.com

www.bluemamba.de
D: alex seifriz   C: alex seifriz   P: alex seifriz
A: alex seifriz   M: bluemamba@bluemamba.de

www.mrdheo.com
D: a4 prod   C: a4 prod   P: a4 prod
A: a4 prod   M: misterdheo@gmail.com

www.tilico.com.br

D: samuel leite, manoel carneiro, jeancarlo cerasoli   C: rogerio goncalves
A: digitale - agência digital   M: contact@digitale.com.br

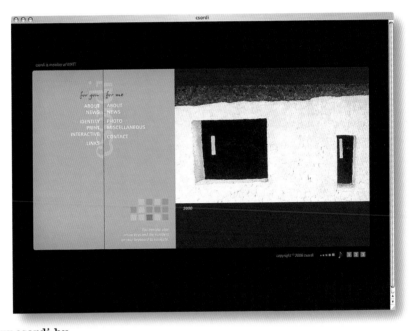

www.csordi.hu

D: zoltán csordás   C: gergely nyikos   P: zoltán csordás
A: csordizájn   M: info@csordi.hu

www.gavinyindesign.com

D: gavin yin   C: gavin yin   P: gavin yin
A: gavin yin design studio   M: info@gavinyindesign.com

www.fabiotamayose.com
D: fábio
M: www.fabiotamayose.com

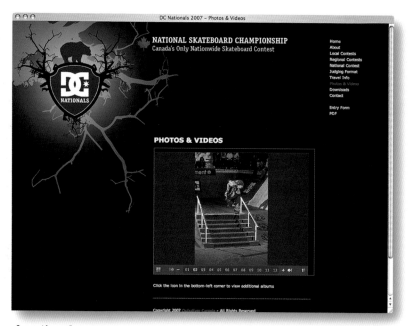

www.dcnationals.com
D: matt lambert   C: matt lambert   P: matt lambert
A: cardeo creative   M: info@cardeo.ca

www.corralmadrigal.com
D: carlos corral-madrigal   C: carlos corral-madrigal
A: baud.es   M: carlos@corralmadrigal.com

www.mifdesign.com

D: myroslav orshak C: sergey lifinsky
A: mif design studio M: www.mifdesign.com

www.benoitb.fr

D: benoit bohnké C: benoit bohnké
M: hello@benoitb.fr

www.nu-gotha.com

D: massimiliano pirotello C: massimiliano pirotello P: emmedueart
A: nu-gotha cinematique M: info@m2art.it

www.dolphin-quays.com

D: lee poynter, nick bain   C: ricardo sanchez   P: jamie sergeant
A: strange   M: jamie@strangecorp.com

www.berghoff.eu

D: timo hunold   C: timo hunold   P: timo hunold
A: hunoldmarketing   M: www.hunold-marketing.de

www.caketheatre.com

D: danny teo   C: danny teo   P: danny teo
A: ace daytons advertising   M: danny@d3zin3.net

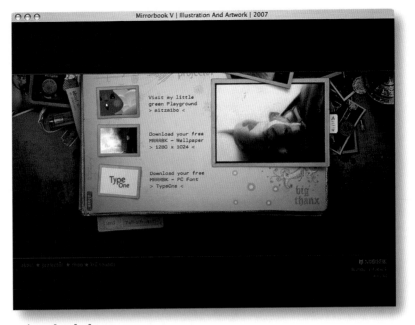

www.mirrorbook.de

D: michael tzscheppan   C: michael tzscheppan   P: michael tzscheppan
A: the mirrorbook   M: info@mirrorbook.de

www.kostry.net

D: bitter lix, krzysztof ostrowski   C: michal balaszczuk   P: bitter lix
A: bitter lix   M: info@bitterlix.com

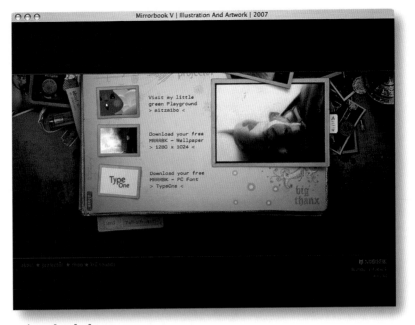

www.madmatcouture.com

D: matt bugeja
A: bma ltd   M: info@bma.com.mt

www.cantinerussotaurasi.com
D: andrea basile   C: basile advertising   P: andrea basile
A: basile advertising   M: info@basileadvertising.com

www.doblerstudio.com
D: ricard rovira   C: ricard rovira
M: info@doblerstudio.com

ghentelmen.com
D: lukas bronisz   C: lukas bronisz   P: lukas bronisz
M: ghente@gmail.com

www.guliveris.lt

D: simonas sileika, vilius sileika   C: simonas sileika

A: "guliveris"   M: info@guliveris.lt

first.pencilrebel.com

D: grzegorz kozakiewicz, patrycja hojna   C: rafal bielec   P: grzegorz kozakiewicz

A: pencil rebel - mixed media web design   M: love@pencilrebel.com

www.imagespost.com.au

D: lee walters   C: lee walters   P: craig wilson

A: freshweb   M: craig@imagespost.com.au

www.liveroom.tv
D: carly merrydew   C: enjoythis   P: enjoythis
A: liveroom tv   M: kate@liveroom.tv

www.marianoklein.com
D: mariano klein   C: mariano klein
M: m@marianoklein.com

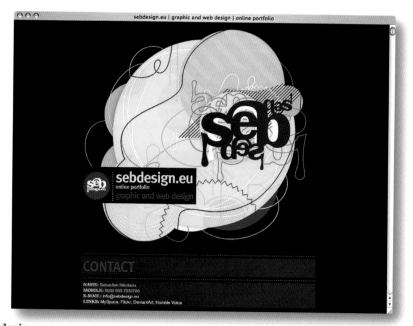

sebdesign.eu
D: sébastien nikolaou   C: sébastien nikolaou   P: sébastien nikolaou
M: info@sebdesign.eu

www.urbtype.com

D: norio ichikawa   C: norio ichikawa, david riegler   P: michelle nguyen
A: urbtype   M: norio@urbtype.com

www.thebookoftags.com

D: dropdrop
M: info@dropdrop.net

www.sumeco.net

D: theo aartsma   C: maikel joey sibbald   P: maikel joey sibbald
A: sumeco.net   M: info@sumeco.net

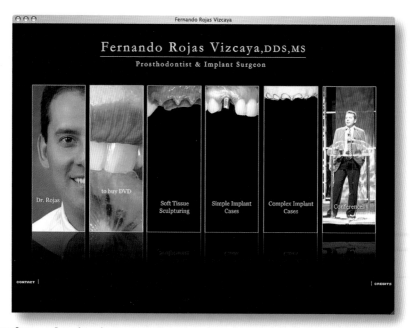

www.fernandorojasvizcaya.com

D: iskiam jara   C: iskiam jara   P: iskiam jara
A: iskiam jara estudio de diseño   M: info@iskiamjara.com

www.shanemielke.com

D: shane seminole mielke   C: shane seminole mielke   P: shane seminole mielke
A: shane seminole mielke   M: shane@shanemielke.com

www.danielsenphoto.com

D: arild danielsen   C: arild danielsen   P: arild danielsen
A: photographer   M: arild@danielsenphoto.com

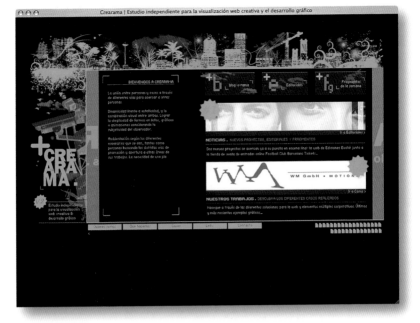

www.crearama.es

D: miguel antolín cubero C: miguel antolín cubero P: miguel antolín cubero

A: estudio crearama M: crearama@crearama.es

www.magika-studios.com

D: oliver rosenthal C: oliver rosenthal P: oliver rosenthal

A: mágika studios M: orosenthal@magika-studios.com

www.jazztona.com

D: xevi vilardell bascompte C: xevi vilardell bascompte P: xevi vilardell bascompte

A: xelu.net M: xevi@xelu.net

www.skop.com/brucelee

D: tim buesing, peter muehlfriedel, gundula markeffsky   C: m. kelly, g. mulzer
A: skop   M: tim@skop.com

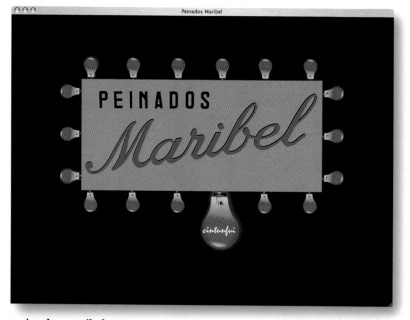

www.peinadosmaribel.com

D: corrales pescador, angel   C: montserrat diaz, enric   P: peinados maribel
A: peinados maribel   M: info@peinadosmaribel.com

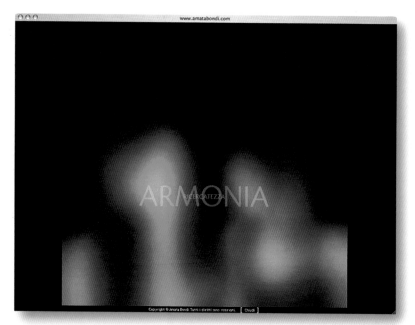

www.amatabondi.com

D: alessio papi   C: alessio papi   P: nextopen multimedia
A: amata bondi   M: www.nextopen.it

www.studio-43.org
D: sergey shinjaev   C: sergey shinjaev   P: sergey shinjaev
A: studio43   M: info@studio-43.org

www.felix-holzer.com
D: richard ajetomobi   C: florian venus
M: mail@felix-holzer.com

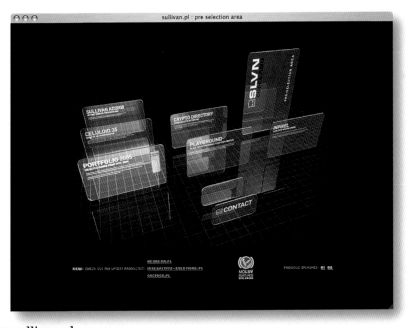

www.sullivan.pl
D: maciej gembara   C: maciej gembara
A: sullivan.pl   M: sullivan@poczta.onet.pl

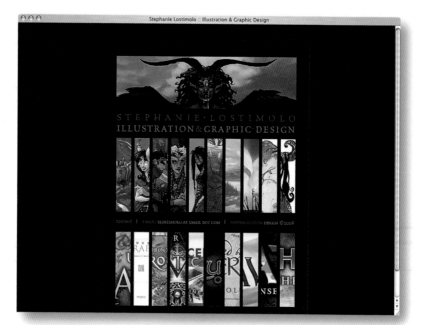

www.lostimolo.com

D: stephanie lostimolo
M: slostimolo@yahoo.com

www.vzwei.com

D: verena jung   C: verena jung   P: verena jung
A: v2   M: welcome@vzwei.com

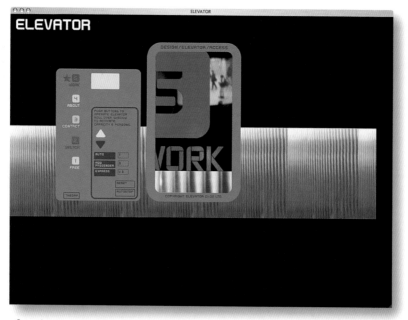

www.elevatoraccess.com

D: liisa salonen, summer powell   C: alex braidwood
A: elevator 01:02 ltd.   M: salonen@elevatoraccess.com

www.popwhore.com
D: yurievi ledesma
M: info@popwhore.com

www.wearethirdeye.com
D: alex di mella   P: david uribe
A: thirdeye design group   M: rosanna@wearethirdeye.com

www.azartmedia.com
D: chris masuy
A: azartmedia   M: info@azartmedia.com

www.thefold.net

D: the fold
A: the fold   M: info@thefold.net

www.locustconstructions.com/karateclub

D: tobias basan   C: tobias basan
M: chopler@gmx.de

www.rareid.com.au

D: peter howie   C: lee borowiak   P: peter howie, mark stewart
A: rare identity   M: info@rareid.com.au

338

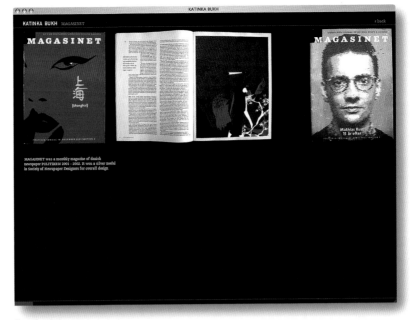

www.katbukh.com

D: anders brødsgaard   C: anders brødsgaard
A: funkybjarne.com   M: anders@funkybjarne.com

www.aurelienducroz.com

D: a. grigoryan   C: g. gadukyan, g. pirumov, s. manukyan   P: stepan aslanyan
A: www.smartsystemsllc.com   M: design@smartsystemsllc.com

www.davidabades.com

D: ana belén álvarez   C: ivan jose mejias   P: rocambolescofilms
A: grapha intuitive   M: www.grapha.net

www.xf-vampires.de

D: christoph kowalski   C: christoph kowalski   P: christoph kowalski
A: christoph kowalski, future visual style   M: info@xf-fx.de

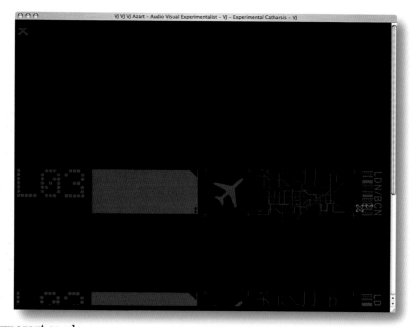

www.azart.co.uk

D: chris masuy aka azart
A: azart   M: azart@azart.co.uk

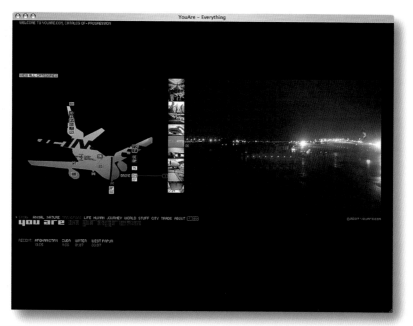

www.youare.com

D: mark craemer   C: mark craemer   P: mark craemer
A: youare.com   M: 1@youare.com

www.lesfemmes.it
D: angelo pariano   C: angelo pariano   P: artedopera, angelo casarrubia
A: lesfemmes   M: info@artedopera.it

www.iamstatic.com
D: ron gervais
M: ron@iamstatic.com

www.lasangreiluminada.com
D: miguel salcedo   C: miguel salcedo   P: martín lópez, eugenio maillefert
A: www.surimimedia.com   M: info@surimimedia.com

www.mattspanky.com

D: martin wolfinger   C: martin wolfinger   P: martin wolfinger
A: martin wolfinger a.k.a. matt spanky   M: office@mattspanky.com

campaign.nokia.com.hk/7500/index.html

D: john chan   C: samson wong   P: postgal.com
A: nokia   M: postgal.com

www.pioneer10.com

D: duane king   C: duane king, darcy brown
A: pioneer10   M: testpilot@pioneer10.com

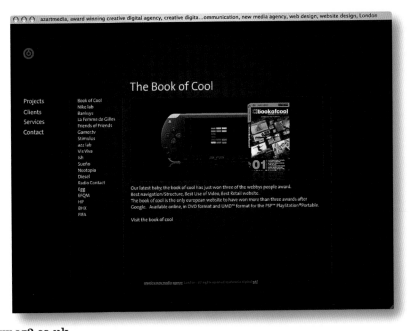

www.az2.co.uk
D: chris masuy
A: azartmedia   M: info@azartmedia.com

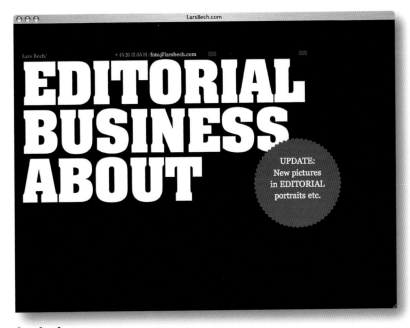

www.punkyfish.com
D: jamie sergeant   C: nick bain   P: ricardo sanchez
A: strange corporation   M: jamie@strangecorp.com

www.larsbech.com
D: thomas høedholt   C: mikkel schultz   P: lars bech
A: das büro   M: foto@larsbech.com

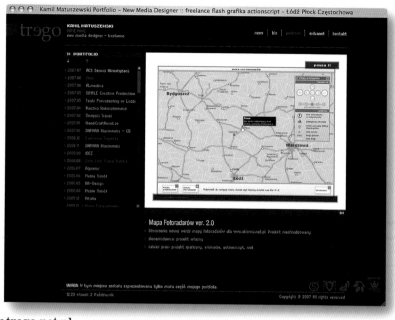

www.trego.net.pl

D: kamil matuszewski   C: kamil matuszewski   P: kamil matuszewski
A: kamil matuszewski   M: kamil@matuszewski.net.pl

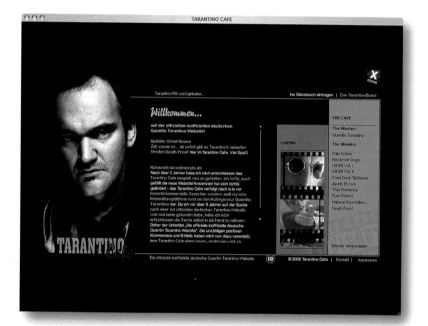

www.tarantinocafe.de

D: benjamin weiss   C: benjamin weiss   P: benjamin weiss
A: b.n.weiss l new york   M: www.bnweiss.com

www.5minutefriend.org

D: matteo cibic
A: matteo cibic   M: info@matteocibic.com

coda.co.za

D: damien du toit   C: damien du toit   P: damien du toit
A: coda.coza   M: webdesignindex@coda.co.za

www.hunold-marketing.de

D: timo hunold   C: timo hunold   P: timo hunold
A: hunoldmarketing   M: www.hunold-marketing.de

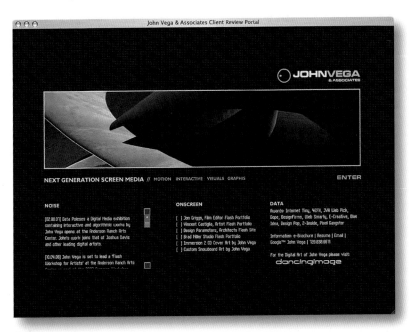

www.johnvega.com

D: john vega   C: john vega, aaron wilson
A: john vega   M: jva@johnvega.com

www.blake-studios.com

D: nico benedict   P: paula babbino
A: blake bw   M: info@blake-studios.com

www.doozers.pt

D: musaworklab   C: musaworklab
A: musaworklab   M: info@musaworklab.com

www.minoflow.com

D: jonathan minori   C: jonathan minori
M: jonathan@minoflow.com

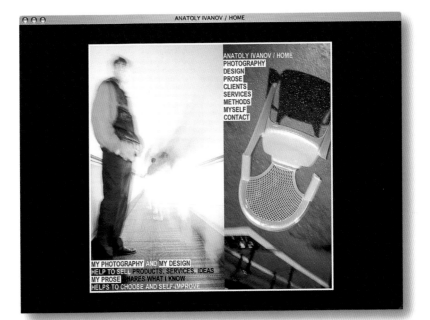

www.anatolyivanov.com
D: anatoly ivanov   C: anatoly ivanov   P: anatoly ivanov
A: anatoly ivanov photography / design / prose   M: info@anatolyivanov.com

www.simonladefoged.com
D: www.funkybjarne.com   C: www.hemper.dk
M: simon@simonladefoged.com

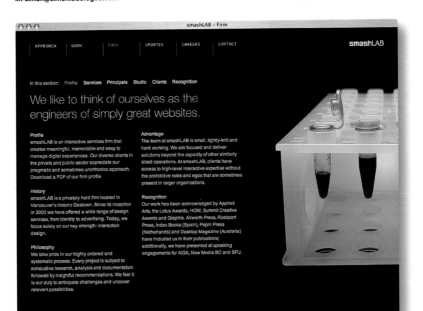

www.smashlab.com
D: eric karjaluoto   C: eric shelkie
A: smashlab   M: karj@smashlab.com

www.gelindomecenero.it

D: samuele schiavo   C: samuele schiavo   P: samdesign
A: samdesign   M: info@samueleschiavo.it

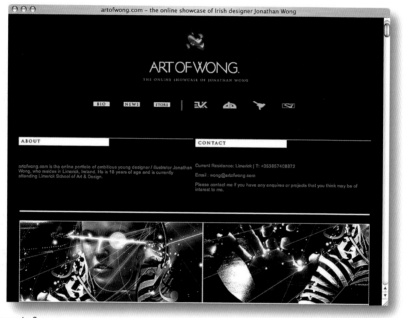

www.artofwong.com

D: jonathan wong   C: jonathan wong   P: jonathan wong
A: artofwong.com   M: wongj10@gmail.com

www.merino200.com

D: lee s walters   C: lee s walters   P: abbie george, brie vogel
A: freshweb   M: sales@freshweb.com.au

www.bettybarclay.com
D: kay köster   C: oliver rutzen, andreas paul, michael castan-lopez   P: collin croome
A: coma2 e-branding   M: collin@coma2.com

www.studiobreakfast.be
D: martin dellicour   C: martin dellicour   P: martin dellicour
A: studio breakfast sprl   M: martin@studiobreakfast.be

www.kaminska.net
D: wojtek lebski
A: www.webski.waw.pl   M: kasia@kaminska.net

www.0-style.com
D: joshua stearns   C: joshua stearns
A: zero style   M: zero@O-style.com

www.sub88.com
D: david vineis   C: sylvain mendez   P: david vineis
A: sub88   M: david@sub88.com

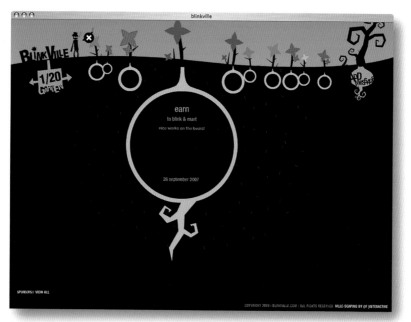

www.blinkville.com
D: liew sanyen   C: kong lee seng   P: blink
A: blinkville   M: sanyen@if.net.my

www.turbulenz.org
D: pascal hoffmann   C: pascal hoffmann   P: turbulenz! visuals
A: turbulenz! visuals   M: visuals@turbulenz.org

www.partyguese.com
D: musaworklab   C: musaworklab
A: musaworklab   M: info@musaworklab.com

www.wozere.com
D: iñigo orduña   C: filippo della casa   P: iñigo orduña
A: imaso   M: info@imaso.net

www.andco.dk

D: pelle martin   C: felix nielsen   P: pelle martin
A: in2media a/s   M: pmc@in2media.dk

www.agriodimas.com

D: julie toth   C: julie toth   P: tommy agriodimas
A: tommy agriodimas photographer   M: tommy@agriodimas.com

www.toshiedo.com.au

D: james mason, toshiedo   C: james mason, toshiedo   P: james mason
A: toshiedo   M: james@toshiedo.com.au

index of designers

index of designers

index of designers

index of designers

index of designers

index of designers

index of designers

index of designers

index of designers

index of designers

index of URLs

index of URLs

index of URLs

index of URLs

index of URLs

index of URLs

Family Law